THE CAVE AND THE SPRING

Also by A. D. Hope

THE WANDERING ISLANDS (Sydney 1955).
POEMS (London 1960, New York 1961).

The Cave
and the Spring

ESSAYS ON POETRY

A. D. HOPE

sed me Parnasi deserta per ardua dulcis
raptat amor; iuvat ire iugis, qua nulla priorum
Castaliam molli devertitur orbita clivo

THE UNIVERSITY OF CHICAGO PRESS

ISBN: 0-226-35155-6 (clothbound);
0-226-35156-4 (paperbound)
Library of Congress Catalog Card Number: 72-116030

The University of Chicago Press, Chicago 60637
The University of Chicago Press, Ltd., London

Contents

Preface

The Cave and the Spring are said still to exist on the mountain sacred to the Muses. I have taken them to stand for several things but principally for the sensory and the verbal imagination respectively. The essays in this book are a random collection of talks and articles produced in the last ten years. They have no necessary connection and make no pretence of scholarship or criticism in the academic sense. They represent a poet's occasional reflections on different aspects of his craft and they are written much as poems are written, to show forth and to illuminate an idea rather than to argue and demonstrate a truth. For this reason they rely more often on appeals to analogy than on analysis and deduction from evidence. As opinions of course they must stand up to criticism on their merits.

A. D. Hope.

Acknowledgments

In their original form, certain of these essays appeared in *Melbourne Critical Review, Prospect, Quadrant, The Southern Review,* and *Twentieth Century.* Acknowledgments are made to the editors of these journals.

Thanks and acknowledgments are offered to authors, editors, and publishers for permission to quote passages from the following: *Christopher Marlowe* by Frederick Boas (Oxford University Press); *The School of Night* by Muriel Bradbrook (Cambridge University Press); *Essays in Poetry* by Vincent Buckley (Melbourne University Press); *The Literary Situation* by Malcolm Cowley (Viking Press); "Tradition and the Individual Talent" by T. S. Eliot (*Selected Essays,* Faber and Faber Limited); *Christopher Marlowe* by Una Ellis-Fermor (Methuen & Company Limited); "The Poet as Hero" by S. L. Goldberg (*Meanjin*); "Imperial Adam" by A. D. Hope (*The Wandering Islands,* Edwards and Shaw, and *Poems,* Hamish Hamilton Ltd); *The Road to Xanadu* by John Livingstone Lowes (Constable and Company Limited); "The Pyramid in the Waste" by James McAuley (*Quadrant,* Vol. v, No. 4, 1961, and *Australian Literary Criticism,* ed. Grahame Johnston, Oxford University Press, 1962); *Safe Conduct* by Boris Pasternak, translated by Alec Brown (Elek Books Limited); and *Poetry Direct and Oblique* and *Five Poems 1470-1480* by E. M. W. Tillyard (Chatto & Windus Limited, London, and Barnes and Noble, N.Y.).

The Discursive Mode

THERE have been many histories of poetry, but its natural history has yet to be written. The fantastic variety and profusion of living forms in nature are all related and depend on one another. The naturalist knows this well and he knows that, while these relations are never simple in themselves, they often depend on a few quite simple natural laws which constitute the science of ecology.

Man is part of nature, and human ecology is a part of general ecology. The arts of man rise and flourish and decay as do the races and species of living things; they are rooted in the mind and heart, they depend on the climate of society in much the same way as plants and animals depend on soil and seasons.

The balance of nature in any region undisturbed by man appears to be relatively constant. Each species of plant or animal has its natural and prodigal fertility kept in check by natural enemies and the limitation of its supply of food. But each species depends on other species for a suitable and protective environment and this becomes apparent when the balance is upset. Disappearance of one species because of the failure of controls on its natural enemies may lead to disappearance of the predators as well. And this may in turn lead to further disturbance of the balance of nature. Destruction of tall timber may lead to the disappearance of many types of undergrowth which it sheltered, and destruction of certain lowly types of plants may lead to leaching of the soil, which leads ultimately to destruction of the major forms of vegetation.

It would be foolish to apply this analogy too closely or too literally to poetry. Poems are not organisms and do not reproduce themselves. But the various forms of poetry do

1

depend on one another in something the same way as the various forms of animal and plant life. They have a natural order among themselves, and neglect of any of the great forms by the poets affects the practice of all the others. The introduction of a new literary form, if it becomes popular, may seriously upset the whole traditional balance of literature. Moreover changes in social structure, in education or in belief, outside the field of literature, may destroy this balance in such a way that certain traditional forms fail to command respect and cease to be practised. This, in turn, weakens the respect for others, for the different forms support one another. One after another the great forms disappear; the remaining forms proliferate and hypertrophy and display increasing eccentricity and lack of control. A general erosion of the mind proceeds with more and more acceleration. A desert ecology replaces the ecology of the rain forest. The forms are few, small, hardy, and reflect the impoverished soil in which they grow. If the process goes a little further a point of no return is reached; sand, clay and naked rock present a lifeless and inhuman landscape where only minimal forms of life persist.

I have seen physical deserts of this kind in several parts of Australia: that made by the intrusion of the goat and the rabbit in South Australia; that produced by the greed and ignorance of too intense cultivation in the Mallee; that produced by poisonous fumes around Mt Lyell in Tasmania. The analogous destruction of the landscape of literature by the intrusion of alien and sterile forms of cheap amusement, by exhaustion of the heart and mind, proceeding from greedy and ignorant exploitation of their resources, and by a poisoning of the atmosphere of belief in which the forms of art breathe and flourish, is an obvious feature of the world in which we live. Looking backwards, it is easy now to see the slow progress towards a desert ecology from the sixteenth century to the present day. It is still a young desert, like parts of the centre of Australia, capable of responding to rain and good seasons or to irrigation, not yet a Sahara or a Gobi. It has its oases. But gone is the landscape in which the epic, the

2

great philosophic poem and the verse tragedy massed their great timbers and delighted by the contrast of forms and foliage; in which verse satire, the ode, the epistle, the elegy, the romance, the hortatory or instructive poem, the pastoral and the long meditative poem or celebrant hymn, gave its general character to the woodland, while innumerable lowlier forms of sonnet or epigram and song filled all the space between. Instead there now is only the sparse and monotonous vegetation of the arid steppe: little poems of reflection, brief comments, interior monologues, sharp critical barks and hisses, songs that never become articulate; earnestness that lacks the enchantment of truth, and frivolity that disgusts by its absence of charm.

The death of the great poem began in the seventeenth century. The balance of nature was disturbed when a new literary form, the novel or, as Fielding called it, the comic prose epic, arose. It is no accident that one died as the other began to flourish. Something noble in the mind of man died with it and something more comfortable and amusing took its place. Verse tragedy no longer supported by the taste for epic declined too, and comedy supported by the novel rose to take its place. The tragic mode gave way to the pathetic. In the eighteenth century, satire became the dominant form, and the disposition of the lesser kinds it sheltered was changed. The profuse varieties of lyric verse disappeared till only the song designed to be sung in the theatre remained. The ode suffered hypertrophy into the grotesque Pindarique. Sham extensions of the *Georgics* celebrated the wool-trade, the cultivation of sugar cane and the art of preserving health. The pigmy shape of mock epic flourished in the space left by epic in exquisite or impotent parody. The great poems of the period were ghosts: Dryden's translation of the *Aeneid*, Pope's translation of Homer. These poets gave life to what they transplanted, but in themselves they were a sign that the impulse to write original epic was gone.

When the long narrative poem was revived once more it was plain that the impulse came now from another source. It is not Ariosto or Pulci that stands behind Byron's *Don*

Juan but the novels of Sterne and Fielding; it is not Milton or Lucretius that give character to Wordsworth's *Prelude* but the *Confessions* of Rousseau and the novels of Henry Mackenzie. Even *The Idylls of the King* is a kind of Victorian fiction in romantic fancy dress. The great narrative poem began to accept its inferiority to the novel and to imitate its methods. Clough and the Brownings went all the way. But the year *The Bothie of Tober-na-Vuolich* appeared was the year of *Dombey and Son, Vanity Fair,* and *Wuthering Heights. Aurora Leigh* appeared between *Little Dorrit* and *The Virginians,* and *Red Cotton Night-Cap Country* on the heels of *Middlemarch.* What chance could they have? The poets had sold the pass to no purpose.

Things now fell apart rapidly and thoroughly. Verse tragedy, which had tried to take the place of epic in the seventeenth century, died a lingering death in the eighteenth and early nineteenth centuries, to be exhumed in the twentieth by writers of recitative which imitates the voice of poetry much as a female impersonator imitates feminine mannerisms. Satire succumbed with Byron. The elegy, the ode, and the verse epistle quietly stopped breathing and nobody noticed their passing. The twentieth century woke up to find that the forest had vanished and only the monotonous mediocrity of the prairie remained.

Just as a certain nobility of mind was lost with the passing of epic from the living forms, just as real magnanimity was lost with tragedy, so one by one the attitudes of mind and heart, which made the use and being of the other great forms, died out as they ceased to be practised. A loss and a limitation of consciousness followed, so that men, whether readers or poets, were unable any longer to understand what they had lost, or indeed what was meant by a 'form' at all. That the power and range of each kind of poetry was intimately related to the structure, the appropriate metres, the formal character of epic, of satire, of ode, or drama, exactly as the character and nature of each kind of plant or animal is the product of its 'form', it was no longer possible to recognize. Men could see nothing but arbitrary or chance types of construction, and they came to the perverse conclusion that these forms, having perished, had nothing to do with the essential nature of poetry. Poetry in its purest form they decided was to be found in the lyric. Edgar Allan Poe propounded the new heresy in an essay which became one of the bases of symbolist doctrine. Narrative, drama, excogitation, argument, description were rejected as having nothing to do with the pure essence of poetry. Poetry was music. Poetry was not the thing said, but continual evocation of delicious suggestions of meaning. Poetry was an unconscious crystallization of glittering images upon the bare twig of metre. Poetry, at the nadir of this search for its essence, became the formless babble and vomit of the poet's subconscious mind.

One thing more disastrous, perhaps, than the disappearance of the great forms, has been the concomitant disappearance of the middle form of poetry: that form in which the uses of poetry approach closest to the uses of prose, and yet remain essentially poetry. It was a form which served without pretension the purposes of narration, the essay, the letter, conversation, meditation, argument, exposition, description, satire or cheerful fun. Its mood, like the mode, was discursive, not intense or elevated or passionate. It was in this middle field that the poets learned the exercise and management of their craft, the maintenance and modulation of tone, the arts of being at once well-bred, elegant, sincere and adept. It was from this middle ground that the poets moved to higher flights, and moved with assurance and skill. And it was from this common ground, this basic level of performance, that public taste was able to measure their progress towards the true sublime and to appreciate lapses of poetic tact, failures, and absurdities, which are largely hidden from the poets and their readers today. It did not depend, like most of the admired poetry of today, on a profusion of startling images, but on the plain resources of ordinary English used with inimitable aptness and animated by metre and rhyme. It was in this middle style that Chaucer wrote his tales, that Jonson could describe Penshurst, the house of his friend and patron, Dryden retell a tale from Boccaccio or argue in *Religio Laici* against the faith he was so soon to embrace, Smart describe the picking of hops in Kent, or Wordsworth relate with quiet amusement his student life at Cambridge. Browning found it ready to hand, the medium of speech neither dramatic nor merely colloquial, yet suggesting both, for his remarkable gallery of men and women. In it he wrote *The Ring and the Book*, the greatest *poem* of the nineteenth century, which, because of its medium, is perfectly effective and yet not great poetry. The discursive mode is not wholly unpractised today. Martyn Skinner has used it in *Letters to Malaya*, and Robert Frost in some of his New England poems, to mention two modern poets. But it has disappeared from what is fashionable and has therefore ceased to be part of the education of young poets and the natural measure and standard, for public taste, of success or failure in the intenser forms of poetry.

One of the masters of the discursive mode in English is Cowper. Few read *The Task* nowadays, but it deserves to be read if only to remind us of the still centre, the simple graces, the unobtrusive ceremony of language, for loss of which the whole natural order of poetic forms has fallen apart:

> *Now stir the fire, and close the shutters fast,*
> *Let fall the curtains, wheel the sofa round,*
> *And, while the bubbling and loud-hissing urn*
> *Throws up a steamy column, and the cups,*
> *That cheer but not inebriate, wait on each,*
> *So let us welcome peaceful evening in.*

In Cowper, in much of Dryden, above all in Chaucer we have the discursive mode at its barest and simplest. Metre and the unaffected skill of the poet draw the natural words and syntax into a movement that constitutes the dance of language we call poetry. On mastery of this basic skill depends the successful use of all the higher resources of poetry. On a taste discriminating enough to appreciate this as poetry, depends the power to discriminate and to appreciate all the higher forms in their appropriate and natural order, and to see them for what they are. Without this principle of discrimination no one can understand the *composition* of a long poem. No long poem can stay always at the height; the poet must understand the art of modulation, and mastery of the discursive mode is the key to this art. On this depend proportion, harmony, connection, surprise, and the power to return without lapsing into dullness—all the architectonic skills. In the possession of this knowledge the poets have no need, as seems to be the case today, of theories of magic or techniques of chance collision or subterranean evocation. The theory of poetry is simply that of the natural use of natural forces to produce effects never known in nature and to make these forces serve ends, not different from those met with in other kinds of social intercourse, but only at a heightened level of perception and a higher organization of heart and mind. And it is in this use of natural forces to new ends that poetry takes its place among the characteristically human and humane occupations.

The counter view, which now holds the field, was enunciated by Poe in 1848:

> I hold that a long poem does not exist. I maintain that the phrase, 'a long poem', is simply a flat contradiction in terms. I need scarcely observe that a poem deserves its title only inasmuch as it excites, by elevating the soul. The value of the poem is in the ratio of this elevating excitement. But all excitements are, through a psychal necessity, transient. . . .
>
> That degree of excitement which would entitle a poem to be so-called at all, cannot be sustained throughout a composition of any great length. After the lapse of half an hour, at the utmost, it flags—fails—a revulsion ensues—and then the poem is, in effect, and in fact, no longer such.

There would be no point in contemplating the ingenious but essentially trivial arguments of Poe's *The Poetic Principle* had these arguments not had the misfortune to justify so aptly what was going on in poetic practice in the nineteenth century, and had they not, by a series of unfortunate accidents, become the basis of so many varieties of modern poetic doctrine. Poe's opinion hardly deserves a serious answer. He might just as well have maintained that love consists only of

7

brief passages of intense excitement in sexual intercourse, and that, because a man cannot prolong these moments indefinitely, he is never in love except when he is in bed. Nothing so well illustrates the disaster which followed the loss of any sense of the nature and the importance of the discursive mode as this tendency to equate poetry with excitement. Poe's essay goes on to proclaim that coherent argument, narrative, and description are irrelevant. Poetry, he makes it seem, elevates us as a bottle of whisky may put us in a state of elevation. If we take more than a little of either 'a revulsion ensues'. A generation which could see no poetry in Pope took the view that the essence of poetry was to be found in Palgrave's *Golden Treasury* of 1861 and 1869.

'Though they may write in verse, though they may in a certain sense be masters of the art of versification, Dryden and Pope are not classics of our poetry, they are classics of our prose,' wrote Matthew Arnold in 1880. Palgrave and Arnold were education officials. Both became Professors of Poetry at Oxford. It may be significant that since their day education in schools, on which the formation of public taste so much depends, has offered as the basis of the study of poetry mainly anthologies of the Palgrave sort, and that the study of poetry in universities so often neglects the discursive mode. We live in a world which has been systematically brought up without appreciation of the plain bread of poetry, which has as systematically had its taste formed on little cakes and sugarplums, to appreciate nothing but short spasms and concentrated sweetness, which has never learned the habits of sustained attention which greater works demand.

When plant ecologists have wished to restore and regenerate the surface of an erosion plain they first planted the dunes with coarse and resistant grasses with roots that bind and stabilize the clay slope along with a hardy succulent—such as pigface. Additional grass and small weeds could then take root on the protected surface. Slowly humus was formed; bacteria and fungi in the humus built up nutrients, fixed nitrogen, and restored the soil until it could support shrubs and bushes, until

8

> ... *last*
> *Rose as in Dance the stately Trees, and spred*
> *Thir branches hung with copious Fruit: or gemm'd*
> *Thir Blossoms: with high Woods the Hills were crown'd,*
> *With tufts the vallies and each fountain side,*
> *With borders long the Rivers. That Earth now*
> *Seem'd like to Heav'n, a seat where Gods might dwell*
> *Or wander with delight, and love to haunt*
> *Her sacred shades.*

In other words they followed exactly the steps which Milton describes in the primal act of creation. But where God simply created, they must plant and tend and water.

The regeneration of the ecology of eroded minds is not as easy as this. But because it is hard it should not be thought to be impossible, and the ecological analogy is perhaps instructive. We must start first with the coarse grasses that bind and protect. The first step in intelligent regeneration of the soil of poetry may well be to re-establish the discursive mode, in particular to restore the practice of formal satire. For good satire not only spreads and encourages an appreciation of basic, simple forms of poetry, it not only nourishes and binds the soil, it is in itself a powerful force to check and to eradicate the destructive forms, the noxious and parasitic growths within a civilization, by making them absurd and contemptible. The evil and incoherence and folly in society are also connected. They rely and depend on one another. Wherever the golden derision or the *saeva indignatio* of satire strikes, it weakens and shakes the forces that corrupt the heart and destroy poetry.

Poetry and Platitude

FROM time to time a modern reader of the great masterpieces of European poetry is conscious of what might be called 'noble platitude' in what they have to tell him. It is an interesting reflection of the expectation of readers in our own age that its own poetry rarely follows the paths of:

> *What oft was thought but ne'er so well expressed*

but is taken to be the more interesting, the more unusual, original and unexpected the thought. To tell people in poetry what they already know to be the case is felt to be a waste of time. Some years ago E. M. W. Tillyard drew attention to the importance of what he called the great commonplaces in poetry and in life:

> The great commonplaces have something mysterious about them as embodying the utmost wisdom of the race. . . . In the world's history a great commonplace is every now and then brought forth and poetry may be concerned in its birth; but those that already exist must be kept alive. They are in perpetual danger of perishing. They have to be re-felt continually and reformulated by human experience. They cease to be true unless continually ratified by fresh expression. It is one of the functions of poetry, the most intense form of speech, to keep these commonplaces alive, in contemporary idiom through the ages.*

One sentence in this is curious: 'They cease to be true unless continually ratified by fresh expression.' No doubt Dr Tillyard did not mean to suggest that what is true ceases to be true unless it is continually restated. He is a civilized man and a scholar. He meant to say, perhaps, that men cease to feel these things as true unless they are said again and again, but unconsciously he expressed what is, in fact, one of the

---

* *Poetry Direct and Oblique,* 1934, pp. 42-3.

oldest and most deep-rooted convictions of mankind—a conviction that is embodied in charms and spells, in many types
of ritual prayers, in name-taboos, in proverbs and gnomic
sayings and the wisdom literature of many peoples. It is this
conviction, so deep in most of us that we are not even aware
that it is there, which lies behind the noble sententiousness
of much traditional poetry where the poet does not hope to
surprise or even to instruct us, but simply to put, in a memorable and striking way, some of the obvious facts of common
experience:

> *There is a tide in the affairs of men,*
> *Which, taken at the flood, leads on to fortune;*
> *Omitted, all the voyage of their life*
> *Is bound in shallows and in miseries.*

> . . . . .

> *Nessun maggior dolore*
> *che ricordarsi del tempo felice*
> *nella miseria.*

> . . . . .

> *Hope springs eternal in the human breast;*
> *Man never is, but always to be blest.*

> . . . . .

> *Nobis cum semel occidit brevis lux*
> *Nox est perpetua una dormienda.*

These are examples that immediately come to mind, examples of the sort of quotations that make up the bulk of
any dictionary of quotations. And such dictionaries are made
up of the things people find so memorable that the quotations
acquire the force of proverbial wisdom. Meeting them for
the first time or recalling them on apt occasions, we perceive
that what is put before us is a commonplace of experience,
and yet that it is a commonplace that commands attention,
a truism that we are willing to consider with pleasure, or at
least a platitude before which we suspend our ordinary aver-
sion to platitude. This is partly due to the skill of the poet.
We will accept from Pope, from Shakespeare, from Dante
what we reject from Martin Tupper or Ella Wheeler Wilcox.
We sense an eye seeing what all men see, a voice saying what

all men say and even what few men would think worth making explicit—and yet that the largeness and comprehensive vision of that eye, the plain mastery and the accent of greatness with which the tongue gives utterance to the obvious, compel assent. We have the same sense of illumination that occurs when we have been led to quite new conclusions. We are surprised into admitting the nutritive virtue of facts which we never had reason to doubt.

But this is not our only reason. For if the facts are found nutritive, it is because they satisfy a natural need and hunger. It is not simply that poetry has made the trite palatable. It is that in these works we are supported by what the ancient gnomic wisdom of primitive peoples was designed to support. Nearly every people has its wisdom literature, collections of proverbs, pithy and sententious sayings, epigrammatic rules for the conduct of life, timely warnings about the fickleness of women, the unreliability of princes, the dishonesty of merchants, and so on. A great part of each such collection consists, in fact, of precepts. Such are the *Proverbs of Solomon*, or the maxims of the Old Norse, *Hávamál*. They make up a considerable part of the two Old English poems called the *Maxims* or *Gnomic Verses*. But, embedded among the precepts and the maxims and the proverbial wit and wisdom of such collections, there is usually an older stratum of sayings which have no apparent point or purpose. In *Proverbs* we find:

> *There be three things which go well, yea, four*
> *are comely in going: A lion which is strongest*
> *among beasts, and turneth not away for any; a*
> *greyhound; and he goat also; and a King, against*
> *whom there is no rising up.*
>
> .   .   .   .   .
>
> *The glory of young men is their strength; and the*
> *beauty of old men is the grey head.*

Examples from the Old English gnomic verses are even more striking:

> *The Hawk shall on the glove,*
> *The wild one, dwell, the Wolf in grove*
> *The wretched and solitary one, the boar in the wood*
> *Stout in the power of his tusks; the good man shall in his land*
> *Gain glory; the javelin shall in the hand*
> *The spear ornamented with gold; the gem shall in the ring*
> *Stand forth wide and high; the stream shall in waves*
> *Mingle with the sea-flood; the mast shall be on the ship,*
> *The sailyard remain; the sword lie on the breast,*
> *The noble iron; the dragon shall be in the mound*
> *Wise, proud of his treasure; the fish in the water*
> *Bring forth its kind; the King shall in the hall*
> *Distribute rings; the bear shall be on the heath*
> *Old and dreadful; the waters from the hill shall*
> *Fare flood-grey; the troops shall go together*
> *In a glorious band; Trust shall be in the earl,*
> *Wisdom in man; the wood upon the earth shall*
> *Bloom with life; the mound on the earth shall*
> *Stand forth green; God shall be in heaven,*
> *Judge of deeds; the door shall be in the hall*
> *The broad mouth of the building; the boss shall*
>   *be on the shield*
> *A firm protection for the fingers: the bird aloft shall*
> *Sport in the air. . . .*

These are not precepts: they are statements of what is the case; they stress what is the most obvious quality of the thing named. Similar series of apparently unrelated statements are to be found in the Anglo-Saxon and Old Norse Runic poems, and epic and religious poetry of the time abounds with such sententious assertions. Scholars see little in these poems but a random collection of observations about nature and society, interspersed with some moral maxims. But it is the very random nature of the observations which is perhaps their point: they mention anything that comes to mind without specific sequence, because they aim at everything in the whole order of being. In the passage just quoted we have, pithily stated, what is the expected, indeed the obvious, thing about all things which duly follow their natures, the hawk in the hand, the boar in the thicket, the ship on the sea, the King on his throne, God in his heaven. These bald truisms seem to us arid and pointless because we have forgotten the attitude of mind that produced them, the state of society for which they had seminal and even judicial force. The belief behind them is one embodied in a number of the wisdom literatures: the notion, either of a creative Word which makes and sustains all things and ordains the order of the world, or even of an actual book in which it is all written down and of which men may possess copies in the form of sacred texts and scriptures. But even without this there is the widespread primitive belief that man has his own part and obligation to maintain the order of the universe by his own efforts. To this his garden magic, his hunting magic, his invocations and spells, his ritual observances and taboos all contribute.

Gnomic literature, rightly seen, is much more than a collection of maxims, the shrewd wisdom of the folk, which it becomes in later times. In origin and essence it is a way in which man carries out his side of the continual responsibility for maintaining the frame and order of the world, from the rising and setting of the stars, the procession of the seasons, the nature of beasts and plants and rivers and seas, the order of society and the behaviour of supernatural beings. They have to be kept going. They do not simply maintain themselves. So these summary and cryptic statements that 'frost shall freeze', that 'ships shall sail the sea', that 'the King shall dispense justice', that 'earls shall be bold', that 'the sea shall be salt', and that 'giants shall dwell in the fenlands', are not merely rules of the game of life which all the players have to know, they are in a sense spells which serve to maintain the common round of things and to preserve them from departing from their essential natures. They have a function similar to those other spells which, by the mysterious virtue in a formula, are able to disrupt the common order to produce unusual or destructive events. We could call them *spells of conservation* and *spells of initiation* respectively. There are also restorative spells.

14

A great deal of modern poetry, as has often been observed of late, attempts to work by a kind of thaumaturgy, or magic. It depends for its effect not on what it says, nor on the associations of words with things, nor on the meaning of the poem in terms of any actual states of affairs, nor on anything that is the case or that is asserted to be the case. It depends rather on a power conceived to lie in the words themselves, to create states of mind which alter, add to, suspend or nullify what is the case. In other words these deep and ancient instincts have made it lean more and more to what I call spells of initiation. It is curious to see that, like the spells of magic, unconsciously it becomes obscure, secretive, riddling in the process. From the mumbo-jumbo of *The Waste Land* to the incantatory logorrhoea of the Surrealists is but a step. The whole bias of the modern movement in poetry has been to make it a form of superstition and a form of superstition whose nearest neighbours were the sinister nonsense of the Black Mass and the insane ravings of the asylum patient.

No doubt, if practised today, the magic of conservation and restoration would be equally superstitious. But with the passage of time and the growth of rational religions this earlier magical aspect of poetry has passed over quite naturally into another form which still serves to feed that hunger of the heart to participate in and support the order of the world. The gnomic element in the European tradition has become the view of poetry as an act of celebration rather than an act of magical underpinning. The poetry of the great commonplaces, the plain poetry of description and statement, the great narrative or the great dramatic poem embodying for its age a restatement of some acknowledged truth, all these things draw part of their delight from the sense in both reader and writer, that they are making an act of celebration —and this is always an act of joy, even when what is asserted is itself a tragic or a terrifying truth. It is this function of asserting what is the case as a conscious and satisfying celebration of the nature of things that modern poetry has largely lost. In losing this it has lost one of its main reasons for existence.

When I speak of celebration, I do not mean that poetry is concerned to be nothing but paean and praise of the natural order. It is much more than this. It involves not only that admiration and delight in what one perceives, which is the essence of praise, but also an intellectual assent to the causes that make the natural world an order and a system, and an imaginative grasp of the necessity of its processes. More than this, it involves a sense of communion with these natures and participation in their processes. It is for the poet to feel himself to be not merely the mirror of nature or its commentator but the voice of creation, speaking for it and as part of it. In that admirable phrase of Bacon in *The Advancement of Learning*, he is God's playfellow.

Solomon the King, although he excelled in the glory of treasure and magnificent buildings, of shipping and navigation, of service and attendance, of fame and renown, and the like, yet he maketh no claim to any of these glories, but only to the glory of the inquisition of truth; for so he saith expressly, 'The glory of God is to conceal a thing, but the glory of the King is to find it out'; as if according to the innocent play of children, the Divine Majesty took delight to hide his works, to the end to have them found out; and as if Kings could not obtain a greater honour than to be God's playfellows in that game, considering the great commandment of wits and means, whereby nothing needeth to be hidden from them.

Though Bacon is here speaking of kings, the function of the poet in this respect is equally royal, and, as a function, it belongs now perhaps more to poets than to kings.

The Three Faces of Love

No one, so far as I know, has thought much about the education of poets in our society. This is hardly surprising in a society which makes no provision for poets even to live. But it is proper for poets to think about it for they have to contrive to survive in spite of their society; and there seem to be reasons for thinking that their education should differ from that of other kinds of artists and from that of other kinds of men.

As far as other artists are concerned, there is no apparent reason why there should not be schools of poetry in which young writers are taught their craft just as painters are trained to paint, sculptors to cast and hew and model, musicians to compose and perform, actors to act, and dancers to dance. Yet when one ponders the question, there seem to be good reasons why poets should always have differed from other artists, in the fact that they conduct their own education in the craft. One reason is that the other arts all involve a physical dexterity which nature does not provide. In each case this physical dexterity, to be of any use, has to be pushed to the point of exquisite control that is required, for example, by champion billiard players or by jugglers, though these professions are not fine arts. In consequence, any painter or musician or dancer has to spend years of concentrated effort under a teacher before he can give even a rudimentary performance of his art. To become an accepted artist, of course, requires further years of independent and intelligent practice. Now little of this preliminary training is needed to become a writer. The physical skill required is negligible and one that all literate people possess. Only in countries like China is calligraphy actually a part of the literary skill, and sometimes the most important part of it.

But there is perhaps a more important reason why writers, unlike other artists, are usually self-taught, and that is the fact that all the other arts manipulate their material, whether it is paint or stone or the muscles of the body, or a musical instrument making audible sounds. Quite apart from the dexterity this manipulation asks for is the fact that it is something the learner can see before him, or hear, or which his teachers can see and hear. A clumsy stroke, an awkward gesture, a false note or badly delivered phrase is immediately obvious. The whole process takes place outside the operator, and the gap between what he meant to do and what he actually succeeds in doing is therefore open to external criticism. But a poet composing a poem is doing it very much more inside himself, in a private world that nobody else can share until he has done it and translated it into words. Writing from the beginning is a solitary process, the material shaped by the mind is the material of the mental life itself.

The last and I think the most important difference of all is that a sort of serious play enters into the business of learning to write very much more than it does in the practice of the other arts—though it does have a place in all of them. Children and young animals train themselves for grown-up life by play which is an end in itself: the essence of much of this play is make-believe. Children playing at hospitals or mothers and fathers are imitating and imagining at the same time. They know that they are not actually being what they play at. So the rules of the game are variable and full of fantasy. Young writers are much the same while they are learning. The game is simply played in the mind instead of on the nursery floor. Bestride a stick and you have a horse and nobody worries that the stick does not look in the least like one. Make up a story about a horse and what you tell yourself is the horse in much the same way that the stick becomes a horse. It is only little by little that you learn to tell a horse story that will be truly and convincingly 'horsey'. But the young painter is only starting to control his pictorial imagination and therefore to be free to let his imagination 'play' at the point when he can make a horse look like a real horse. One might say that in painting, skill releases the imagination; in writing, a released imagination leads to discovery of the skill.

But if poets, in common with other writers, need a different kind of education in their craft from that needed by other sorts of artist, it is also, I think, true that in common with other artists they need a different sort of education from that which society generally provides. They need in fact an education based on a recognition of the fact that theirs is a mode of life different from that of other men. Before this can happen society must recover a sense of different modes of human life. I am not concerned with the ways in which the occupations of men can be classified into trades and professions or callings. Nor am I primarily concerned with the psychological divisions of men into well-marked types, nor with special gifts and abilities, though these have some bearing on my subject. The social and the psychological aspects of man occupy so much of the attention of modern science that what I call the properly philosophical aspect of man tends to be overlooked or neglected even among philosophers. Yet it was once a matter of prime concern to consider human life as a subject for metaphysical inquiry and not simply as material for empirical research and generalization in the fields of social and psychological science.

What I mean by the modes and kinds of human life, is the kind of thing that St Thomas Aquinas is discussing in the one hundred and seventy-ninth question of the Secunda Secundae Partis of the *Summa Theologica*. The question is divided into two parts in which St Thomas first asks whether life is fittingly to be divided into active and contemplative, and second, whether this division is adequate or not. To both he answers: Yes. My object is to ask and answer the same double question, though I shall not conduct the argument in scholastic or Aristotelian terms and I shall, with great regret, have to dispense with the charming type of argument, to which St Thomas gives some, though not the chief, weight: the argument that, since Leah and Rachel in the Old Testament, and Mary and Martha in the New, symbolize the active and the contemplative life respectively, this is the proper

19

division—otherwise one must suppose that God would have given Jacob three or more wives and Lazarus three or more sisters.

In my own mind, the idea itself did not actually start from what St Thomas has to say about the active and the contemplative life. It began from a consideration of what Dante has to say about the nature of love in the eighteenth canto of the *Purgatorio*. In the previous canto Virgil has been explaining to Dante the nature of Purgatory, the nature of sin, and the nature of love. Love is what moves anything in the direction of another, not only man to his kind and man to God, but the stone towards the ground when it falls, or the fire towards the sky as it burns. Dante asks for further information and definition of the nature of this universal force. Virgil explains that the mind is created with a special aptitude or tendency to love. When it is stimulated by an object pleasing to it, it creates within itself an impression or image of the object, and if the mind inclines towards the object, that inclination or movement of the mind is what Virgil defines as love.

> Then even as fire moves upward by reason of its form, whose nature it is to ascend . . . so the mind once captivated enters into desire, which is a spiritual movement, and never rests until the object of its love makes it rejoice.

Later in the same discussion he explains that man does not know the sources of the natural appetites in himself which make love possible: 'They are in you,' he says, 'just like the instinct in bees to make honey.' It was from these two hints that I began thinking about the modes of love in scholastic terms in which they can still, to some extent, be validly distinguished.

In the first place, as we are concerned with man, we can accept the controversial notion of a final cause. Because men, unlike stones or moths, are conscious of themselves and the world about them, because they have memory and intelligence, they can propose to themselves ends of action which then become causes of their behaviour, though these ends may be far in the future and may even be illusory or imaginary.

The ends that men propose to themselves arise from their impulses and desires, and these in turn are determined by the natures of the men who have them. Because he is conscious, man is able to know his own nature and his own desires and to choose between them. Unlike the stone or the moth his actions and pursuits can be free in so far as he submits them to the intellect, that is to say, in so far as he knows all the conditions of choice implied by the conditions of his own nature and that of the world he lives in. Unlike the lower animals, his impulses are not specific, nor, as instinctive urges are, tied to specific predetermined ends. He is free therefore to propose to himself any end within the range of his knowledge.

Nor is his knowledge limited, as that of animals probably is, by the range of objects which his practical ends dictate. Knowledge, no doubt, arises in the first place as a device of the organism for the better pursuit of its practical ends. But it develops beyond this precisely because the human organism lacks specific instinctive mechanisms such as those of nest-building. Because the objects of human knowledge are not tied to such specific mechanisms, nothing in the range of possible knowledge is irrelevant to the successful attainment of man's practical ends, and this is the means of freeing knowledge from practical ends altogether.

Thus we see in man what so often occurs in nature, the extension or transference of functions for which certain organs and organization have been developed to other purposes which the same organs serve. The most remarkable case of this is perhaps the organs of the tongue, mouth, larynx, lungs, and nose. Originally developed for the intake of food, drink and air, they have developed a secondary function as the organs of speech. Similarly with the organ of knowledge and consciousness, the brain; originally evolved to improve the creature's ability to pursue its practical ends of survival, there has developed in man, perhaps from an original animal curiosity such as we see in monkeys, an independent faculty of knowing for its own sake the contemplative intellect. The intellect is now not simply a faculty which draws its prime urge from the need to acquire food, or love, or power. It has its own specific impulse: *to know*, and its own specific desire, as specific as hunger or sexual desire or the desire to dominate, and its own specific pleasure or gratification, which is the pleasure or joy of contemplation of the objects of knowledge. And just as the power of speech opens a whole new range of powers to the formerly speechless animal, so the emergence of the free or contemplative intellect opens a new range of powers and possibilities to the human creature. It is, in fact, what differentiates him most from other animals. It is his distinguishing human characteristic.

The activities of men, therefore, can be satisfied in two principal ways: by the possession of the objects of desire or by the contemplation of these and of all the other possible objects of knowledge. This is the valid basis of the distinction between the active way of life and the contemplative way of life. The two ways of life are naturally not mutually exclusive. Contemplation is itself an activity and may involve continual active striving to attain its ends as it does in science and scholarship. Nor is it a stasis, for the fruition of knowledge always raises the possibility of further knowledge, and the pleasure of contemplation always contains in itself the urge to know further. Active life continually demands the results of contemplative knowledge to achieve its practical ends. Because man is a complex creature endowed with both sorts of urge, he cannot in any case avoid being both active and contemplative. The philosopher who neglects to provide a means of eating will soon cease to be able to pursue philosophy. It is the sort of fruition that each aims at which differentiates the active from the contemplative man.

It is because, in the first place, any man has only limited time to spend in the world that he is forced to choose among his possible activities. In the second place, while all men may feel both sorts of urge, some have a special gift or ability, similar to the special gifts of creative genius, which disposes them to concentrate their energies either on active ends or on contemplative ends. Below the ranks of the chosen, of those with a special genius for one or the other which we see in the great sages or the great men of action, there is a second class of men who are aware that to do a thing supremely well, or to achieve one end to the fullest extent, they need to sacrifice everything else to that end. The first class are the chosen, the second class those who choose to follow one way of life as much as possible to the exclusion of the other. There is therefore a sound basis for St Thomas's division of the types of human life into two sorts distinguished by the nature of the ends they pursue, though we may agree that for the majority of men there is a third way of life which combines the two in varying degrees. We cannot all be specialists, and it would be a serious thing for society if we were

Just as there are the two sorts of life, with their two sorts of end and fruition in view, so there are, in St Thomas's sense, two corresponding sorts of love, each with an initial and a final stage. One may love a beautiful woman and desire to possess her. Her beauty awakens the desire to possess her and the process of attracting her attention, then her interest, and finally the response of love often takes a long time, and is a complex practical activity. During this time the man is said to be *in love*. In spite of the miseries of lovers on which the poets have so much to say, being in love is an exciting and a pleasurable state. But the gratification and fruition of love is the end proposed, and when it comes it is an altogether different and a better sort of happiness. This is an instance of the active life. But there is another sort of love of which the beauty itself is the object, and the fruition and gratification consist in its contemplation. This is closely allied to the contemplative pleasure we take in music or painting or in the observation of nature. In contemplative activity there are also two stages of gratification which are more clearly seen in the pursuit of knowledge than in the contemplation of beauty. The process of getting to know is itself pleasurable, a form of love, but the fruition of the process is to hold and reflect on what one knows in its completeness, and this, like the fruitions of the active life, is a higher and intenser gratification. We could give the first the name of Science or Knowledge, and the second the name of Wisdom. In this age we are so used to thinking of knowledge or the pursuit of science as a means to an end, that the notion of wisdom as an end in itself, the proper end of the contemplative life, has almost been lost from view. The contemplative life itself is associated in most people's minds with yogis and hermits, mystics and recluses—characters whose occupations suggest withdrawal from life rather than the pursuit of wisdom which is nothing less than the crown of life in all completeness.

My main purpose, however, is to suggest that there are not two but three main *ways of life* which together comprise all the modes of man's existence. The third way of life I should call the *creative way*. It is distinguished from the others in the same manner: by a distinct relation of man to the ends he proposes and desires and by a distinctive emotion which attends the pursuit and the fruition of those ends. As the mark of the active way of life is to possess the objects of desire, and the mark of the contemplative way of life is to enjoy the knowledge of the objects of desire, so the mark of the creative way of life is to bring new objects of desire into being. Those who have this gift or urge have it, as Dante says, as bees have the instinct to make honey. The composers of music, painting, poems, and dances do not compose these things in order to possess them or to contemplate them, but rather in order that others may be able to possess them and contemplate them. Once created, of course, the works of art and imagination may become objects of active or contemplative desire like any other existing objects, even for their creators, but these are not the desires that bring them into being. Creation is a separate mode of human activity, and, with those who have the gift, it constitutes a third and distinct way of life. And like the other ways of life it has its own separate and distinct sorts of pleasure, that which attends the process and that which consists of joy in fruition—its own mode of love. Jacob really should have had three wives and Lazarus three sisters.

If we ask why St Thomas did not recognize this third mode, the answer should probably take two forms, though they are related answers. In the first place, St Thomas, though he was a poet, did not pay much attention to art, and took little trouble to find a place for it in his metaphysical system. Creation is for him an attribute of God and not of man— creation, that is, in the sense of the power to create something new that never existed in the world before. In the second place, he apparently follows Aristotle and the Aristotelian tradition in regarding art as a species of imitation and as being concerned therefore with the representation of things already existing in the world. God is the only creator *ab initio*. The creation of works of art would therefore come under the head of the active life, as the enjoyment of works of art would come under that of the contemplative life. But the essential difference, as I have already pointed out, is this —that the writer of a poem or the composer of a symphony has, as his end, neither possession nor contemplation, but the bringing of a new sort of thing into the world. The poet or the painter may indeed give us recognizable likenesses of the forms of common experience; to this extent they use imitation as a means to their further ends. But the poem or the painting in itself is a thing in itself and not an imitation of anything any more than the symphony is an imitation of anything already in the world. It is *sui generis*, a new creation, and belongs to a different order of being from anything it imitates. W. B. Yeats speaks of the poets as people whose work exists not primarily to help or to inform us. When we read them, he says, we 'have added to our being, not to our knowledge'. It is the impulse to 'add to being' which is the distinctive mark of the creative way of life.

This excursus into a neglected field of human philosophy may seem no more than a mental exercise undertaken for its own sake. But it has a direct bearing on the modern world because of the sort of education we impose on all our citizens. In the first place, it is a uniform sort of education for everybody. In the second place, it is specifically designed for the way of life which is bound to be led by nearly everybody—what I described earlier as the mixed way of life, which inevitably has a bias towards the active life. It is largely dominated by practical ends. In the third place, it is subtly permeated by the view that because Jack is as good as his master, there is a taint of privilege and exclusiveness in providing a different sort of education for people with special gifts and powers. Education in the past was not very specific in preparation for the work of the world and because it was limited to a few, it was aristocratic in its temper. But modern education is democratic in temper and becomes yearly more specific in its adjustment of educational needs to social ends. In the past the people destined to devote themselves as fully as possible to one way of life were able to struggle through to their achievement more or less successfully. Today the more excellent and effective their education, the more they tend to be diverted from their true bent, particularly in the cases of the contemplative life and the creative life. In the past, a universal church provided an open door for anyone who felt in himself a gift for the contemplative life, and it was able to provide a discipline and a training to help him attain it. But now the church opens this door only to its own members and more and more citizens are left with none. The very idea of the contemplative life hardly enters into secular education at all. In the universities nobody talks about wisdom any more and the ideal is often a narrow research in which the end in view is nearly always the practical applications of the knowledge acquired.

In the field of creative energies things are perhaps a little better. The purely imitative view of art which dominated Europe to the end of the eighteenth century has gone, but the arts seem to have lost purpose, direction, and coherence with their traditions. The arts are fostered and discussed as never before and yet the works of genius comparable to those of the past somehow fail to appear. This is particularly true of the art of poetry.

If one asks what is wrong I think that one important

answer lies in the sort of education we provide. Our education, as I said, is specific. It aims at turning out well-moulded definite characters which will fit without friction into the society that provides this education. Whether it succeeds in this is not important. The important thing is that this sort of thing might be quite the wrong sort of education for an artist, whose vocation for the creative life may need quite another approach. What most people need to cope with their world is perhaps the training of positive capability. Because the end is known, the means can be adapted to it. But what the artist needs, beyond training in the technical skills necessary for his craft, is not positive capability but what Keats called *negative* capability. This is how Keats describes it in one of his letters:

> I had . . . a disquisition with Dilke, on various subjects; several things dove-tailed in my mind, and at once it struck me what quality went to form a Man of Achievement especially in literature and which Shakespeare possessed so enormously—I mean *Negative Capability*, that is, when a man is capable of being in uncertainties, mysteries, doubts, without any irritable reaching after fact and reason.

In a later letter he continues the description:

> As to the Poetical Character itself . . . it is not itself—it has no character—it enjoys light and shade; it lives in gusto, be it foul or fair, high or low, rich or poor, mean or elevated—it has as much delight in conceiving an Iago as an Imogen . . . A Poet is the most unpoetical of anything in existence because he has no identity—he is continually in for—and filling some other Body—the sun, the moon, the sea and men and women who are creatures of impulse, are poetical and have about them an unchangeable attribute—the poet has none; no identity.

It is precisely because the end of the creative life is something not predictable, something unknown and truly creative, that artists need the sort of education that allows them to

27

develop negative capability, as much as possible, and that our sort of education is unsuited to them.

The essential thing about education for the creative life as distinct from education for the active or the contemplative life is this: that what is truly autonomous must be self-initiating, or it stops being autonomous. For the active life the ends in view are practical ends which depend for their formulation on the known facts about man and society. The form that education for the active life should take can therefore be determined in advance. Similarly for the contemplative life the world as it exists is its object and perhaps God in so far as he is knowable. The conditions of the contemplative life can therefore be set out in advance. But the ends of the creative life can only be surmised, and the great difference between its conditions and the other two modes of human existence is that what is truly creative must create itself. This is the axiom on which any view of education for the creative life must be based.

One of the tasks of a revived philosophy of man would be to re-examine and restore to public consciousness the basic notion of the ways of life as I have described them and particularly to restore the sense of the true nature of the contemplative life and the creative life. The active life is perhaps well enough provided for and can, by its very nature, take care of itself.

The Activists

SOME time ago I was asked by the organizers of a body calling itself the Australian and New Zealand Congress for International Co-operation and Disarmament, to help sponsor a Festival of Arts, which was to form part of the Congress. I refused to take part, not for the political reasons which caused some of its sponsors to withdraw, but because I said that I could see no point in a Festival of the Arts as a contribution to a political campaign, however worthy its aims. Part of the Festival was to be a series of competitions with prizes for painting or sculpture, literary work, and musical compositions. In the original proposals it was suggested that these prizes should be given for the works which were judged most efficacious in promoting the cause of world peace. In my reply I said that I could conceive a poem or a picture achieving this, though I thought the fact that it did so was quite irrelevant to its value as a work of art, but I asked to be informed how the judges would proceed to judge whether a quartet for strings contributed to the cause of peace or not, and how they would decide, among several entries, which musical composition was the most peace-promoting. I received no answer to this point and I would still like to know whether there is, in fact, an answer.

What I call Activism in Literature is most obvious in the field of politics and social theory, but it may take many forms: religious, educational, scientific, patriotic, or just vaguely progressive. In essence it requires the writer to write in such a way that he promotes something. It tells the writer that he has a duty to society beyond the duty of merely being a good writer. Activist criticism always applies a double standard. It asks of a poem for example, not only the ordinary critical question: Is this a good poem? But, according to the view the critic wishes to see promoted, such questions as these: Is it a poem that presents or furthers the democratic

29

way of life? Is it a poem that embodies a genuine Australian outlook? Is it a moral poem? Is it a Christian poem? Is it a poem that tells the truth about human relations? Is it a cultural poem? Is it a poem that conforms to the latest critical theories, or to a progressive literary movement? Is it a poem that will make people kinder to dumb animals? If the answer is *No*, then the poet is felt to have failed in his duty. He is one of those irresponsible people who write poetry simply for its own sake. He is felt to lack a social conscience. If the answer is *Yes*, comparatively mediocre work is apt to receive approval that it does not deserve. The abysmal dreariness of most anthologies devoted to the work of Social Realist writers, Progressive writers, Catholic writers, Australian writers, and so on, is partly due to this confusion of standards in the minds both of their editors and of the writers themselves.

But the instances I have mentioned are comparatively feeble and ineffective attempts to harness Blind Samson to the Philistine mill. Much more insidious in our own age is a growing sentiment for Culture: Cultural Activism is the sort of thing that induces writers to club together to promote *themselves*; to gather in conventions and discuss the state of literature at international conferences, to put pressure on governments to encourage culture, to indulge in the cultural corroborees called Festivals of the Arts. It is more insidious because any writer who is worth his salt can see the difference between what his demon drives him to do and what the promotion of democracy or realism or a theology requires of him, but the promotion of literature, or of the Arts or of Culture in general, is a trap that he more easily falls into because he naturally wants people to read his books and he naturally feels that they will be more cultivated, more 'cultured', if they do, and then, of course, he can write more books. So he takes part in Festivals of the Arts with the pathetic hope that he will help himself and his fellow writers to make the public appreciate him. On the whole, the sight of Blind Samson making sport for the Philistines is more depressing than the sight of him grinding their corn.

The weakness of those who abhor and reject Activism is

that they usually fall back on some form of the theory of Art for Art's sake. They try to persuade us that art has its own ends which are sufficient in themselves, and this may be true. But they make the mistake of trying to persuade us that the artist has no business to promote anything at all and that if he tries to do so his work will be the worse for it. This puts them in an absurd position because so many of the greatest works of literature have a perfectly deliberate social or religious or intellectual purpose. *The Canterbury Tales* does not try to promote anything; nor does *Antony and Cleopatra* or *Wuthering Heights*. But the greatest poem in the English language sets out to justify the ways of God to Man; *The Faerie Queene* has as its avowed intent to educate a gentleman in the moral virtues and *Tom Jones* was written as a counterblast to sentimental lower-middle-class morality. The whole field of satire would be excluded if it is agreed that good literature cannot be tendentious. Yet *Gulliver's Travels, The Dunciad, The Way of the World* and *Don Juan* are some of the glories of English literature. The example of satire is an interesting one because it makes it impossible to argue that some works of literature are great in spite of their tendentious purpose. The great satires are not just great poems, novels or plays which happen to have a social purpose. They are great precisely because they are great as *satires*. And to say they are satires is to say they have a social purpose.

The heresy of Activism is not to be combated by asserting that a work of art can or should have no purpose outside itself, which is plainly not true. It is to be combated by pointing out, on evidence, that great art can have every possible kind of social, moral or intellectual purpose, or it can have none at all. To require all writers to have a particular sort of social purpose has therefore nothing to do with the standards or purposes of literature as such. The argument about purposes is irrelevant. It is not that having a purpose or lacking one will determine whether writing will be good or bad; it is that prescription of purposes which the writer does not find for himself by free election is the best way to ensure that standards will be confused and writing will be mediocre and dull for the very reason that it induces a servile attitude in the writers themselves. It is the nature of the servile to serve, not to lead. It is the nature of the creative to create, to invent, to explore, in a word to lead and not to follow. A man may assent to a creed or a belief which he has not invented for himself. He may put his art to the service and the promotion of that belief and he may write a great book. But the important thing is that he must make that choice himself and not because his party makes it for him. The evil of Activism is that it fosters the view that the party makes the decisions and the writer finds the ways and means. Hence the feeling I have in reading most of the products of the Social Realist school: that I am in a world of servile minds, even when these minds are obviously sensitive and competent at their job. I have the same feeling when my fellow writers try to persuade me to attend some cultural congress or some conference of writers at which they will read one another papers on 'The Place of Literature in the Modern World', or 'The Function of the Writer in Society' or any of the other disgusting topics which are properly the tedious hunting ground not of poets and dramatists but of social scientists and psychologists.

Freedom of choice, which Activism in any form denies to the writer, is essential to real creation for a reason which is not so much that a writer should be able to choose what he is to write and how he is to write. This is important enough. But it is more important, indeed it is crucial, that a writer should be able not to choose, but to be chosen by something in him which he can neither foresee nor predict, something whose nature he can only discover in the process of writing it.

That great nineteenth-century romantic, Karl Marx, once struck a blow against the cruder sort of Activism in literature. A woman writer sent him a novel written to promote the victory of the masses in the class struggle. Marx had a wide and catholic taste in literature and he found the book wretched stuff. But he was a kind man and he sent it back to the writer with some gentle but sound advice. The best way for her to help in the class struggle he suggested was to keep out of it. Not to write for the proletariat or against capitalism, but simply to write about people, an ordinary novel which truthfully depicted men and women and their personal and social relations to one another, to write, in fact, just like the great bourgeois novelists. The truth of the picture was what mattered: the truth did not have to be promoted, it only had to be told.

This was an excellent lesson, though it must have disappointed the lady. In a sense all great literature makes itself known as such by the overwhelming conviction of truth that it produces: either that enlargement of experience which astonishes us with a quite new vision, or that refashioning of experience which Shelley calls the power to strip 'the veil of familiarity from the world and lay bare the naked and sleeping beauty'. But even Marx had his limitations'. His lesson was effective against a crude manifestation of Activism. It failed to strike at the root. I believe that the root is what we have come to call the imitation theory of art: the theory that it is the nature and function of art to tell us the truth about the world in which we live: to inform us, and by informing to instruct and delight.

This view of Aristotle's is not necessarily an activist theory, though it may look like it. The poet need not aim at instructing or educating us any more than a potato aims at providing us with food. But by producing what it is natural to him to produce he may do it just the same. Indeed this is what the best poems do. The trouble with the imitation theory of literature is that it is both true and not true, or not completely true. The world in which we live, the forms of that world and particularly the human part of the world are the subject matter of poetry. It is what poems are about. And as long as we define literature only in terms of what it is about we shall be in danger of falling into the activist fallacy in one form or another

We must define it partly in terms of what it is about or we shall end in some queer verbal parallel to abstract painting. Literature has to be about something, or it is only a gabble of words. But what literature *is*, is not entirely what it is *about*. And when we have seen this the basis of Activism vanishes.

At this point we may return to the idea of a string quartet to promote the cause of peace. This is absurd because music is not an imitation of anything in the natural world. Aristotle thought it was, but his argument is neither clear nor convincing. Because music is not an imitation of anything, it is not *about* anything outside itself. It is what it is and that is enough because it is beautiful and meaningful in itself. What it *is*, is what it is about. It introduces into the world a new kind of thing which does not exist anywhere else in nature. Its material is the musical scale which is a human invention.

Poetry uses as its material not words as sounds alone, but words as meaningful sounds. These structures of rhythm and sound which we call poems signify things other than themselves, unlike the structures of sound and rhythm we call works of music. Poetry is therefore an imitative art in the sense that it signifies things in the world of nature which do or might exist. But it is not *merely* imitative or representational. Like a sonata it consists in itself of a structure which is not a representation of anything in nature, though the elements of which this structure is composed may be representations, or as we more usually call them, *images*. A good poem in this sense is like a fine wine. It is made from objects occurring in nature, but it transforms them into something *sui generis*, so that we do not criticize a wine in terms of its success in conveying to our palates the qualities of fresh and unfermented grapes.

The analogy with wine is not exact enough; whereas the original elements are not recognizable in the wine they are in poetry. The extraordinary thing about poetry is that a transmutation as complete as that of wine from grapes occurs and yet the original elements remain and indeed are seen and felt with greater clarity and intensity than when we meet them in ordinary experience. Poetry therefore is not merely a means to comprehension of the world. Literature is not indeed primarily a representative art at all though it is also a representative art. Primarily and essentially it creates by means of its material something as completely *sui generis* as music creates. Nothing remotely resembling a Mozart concerto occurs in nature. The composer adds a new order of being to the existing orders of nature. And so does poetry. The heresy of Activism is fundamental because it considers only the representational function of literature. By ignoring that aspect of literature in which its essential nature is similar to that of pure music, it is able to argue speciously that the value of literature lies in its use to promote programmes of social change or moral improvement.

In so doing it diverts and degrades the real task of the arts in the world. What this task is, may again be indicated by an analogy which is something more than analogy because it is taken from the earlier stages of what is essentially the same process of the emergence of one order of nature from another.

The analogy runs something as follows: at one time there was a stage in the earth's history when the surface of the land was a desert. It was a desert not because it could not support life but because there was as yet no life to support. Then from the most primitive forms of life the lowliest plants appeared and began to cover the surface with variegated green; and from these the higher forms of plant life, the ferns and grasses, and finally the flowering plants and trees emerged and transformed this earlier barren world. It was a new order of nature. Other new and higher orders of nature emerged in their turn and again transformed the world: the animals, the insects, and finally the mammals and man. Man himself with his new type of intelligence, his power to look before and after, his higher form of consciousness, formed a new order of nature. And out of this order of conscious and intelligent minds there began the first lowly forms of creative art. In the last few thousand years the emergence of civilized societies has made possible the evolution of the fine arts as we know them—creative processes, no longer tied to the practical ends of human societies, no longer serving the needs of society, but served by society which in a sense exists to make them possible, and valuable to men not because they serve practical ends but because through them the mind emerges into a higher level of experience than is possible without them. The arts establish another plane of being, a new natural order in the world. This is the task of the arts, then, to grow, to evolve new forms, to spread over the barren landscape of merely social man the mantle of their rich and various vegetation, to transform that world by filling it with a higher order of creation. Activism is the enemy of this task, because it tries to substitute for it the task of serving the lower order of creation, and promoting its ends, political change, education, culture, Christian morals, or Soviet morale. Under this sort of pressure the poets are like vintners diverted from their primary task of transforming grapes into wine because, socially speaking, grape-juice is healthier for you. So it is, perhaps, but it is a damnably insipid drink—as insipid as most activist literature.

Because writers have the world as their material they are not isolated from the pressures the world brings to bear on them. Because they are men and citizens they share the problems of men in general. The problems of the world are part of their material. But the world should leave them alone if it expects them to carry out their real task. What this task is may be shown in a fable.

The fable is suggested by that great picture by Titian which hangs in the National Gallery in London—*The Meeting of Bacchus and Ariadne in Naxos*—a picture so famous that everyone, I suppose, has seen reproductions of it.

Ariadne decided to help Theseus and save him from the Minotaur; to do this, she knew, she must defy her father, betray her country, flee with a stranger and begin a new life; one can imagine her counting the risk, wrestling with doubt, remorse and guilt, and a natural fear of the consequences. Perhaps it was the first time in her life she had been called on to take a quite irrevocable step, fraught with possible disaster and certain to hurt and harm. In such a situation she would, as anyone would, try to picture the unknown future, life in a stranger nation with other customs and with a man she loved but hardly knew. What she was about to do was terrible to picture and to contemplate, but it could hardly have been beyond the ordinary gifts of imagination. What actually happened to her, however, was.

What Titian has caught so well in his picture is the expression on her face when, finding herself deserted by the man she loved, still following him desperately along the high shore—his ship is still not far away—and not yet sure whether she has been deserted or is merely the victim of an accident, she turns half-way from the prospect of the ship on the sea, to notice the god leaping from his car to seize her. On her face is the expression of the moment when one sees something as *actual* which the mind has not yet grasped as even possible. The spectator sees the whole scene. He sees Theseus and all that he has meant to her as being already in the past, a mere prelude to the life that is about to begin for her. But she knows nothing of this; she is still in the middle of her disaster, and her apotheosis just beginning is a mere intrusion of meaningless accident.

I use this picture as a fable of the difference between genius in literature and mere talent. Some talent remains at home and embarks on no wild adventures. It is effective, able, necessary, and composes the great bulk of the writers and artists in any generation. Rarer and greater talent is adventurous, and proposes to itself new and sometimes perilous experiments and discoveries. But it proposes no more than it can plan and imagine. The quality of real genius is shown in this: that having planned and proposed adventures far beyond ordinary powers and talents, it tends to find that what it imagined and proposed merely serves to free the heart from home influences and habits, its plans serve merely as a prelude to something beyond any possible anticipation—so much so that this has often been described as a divine intervention or inspiration: the descent of divine energy into the human agent.

Activism, by trying to limit the artist to proposed ends and agreed means, belongs to the forces that persuade Ariadne to stay at home.

Free Verse: A Post-Mortem

FREE verse has not died out. It is, I believe, happily on the decline, and few serious poets now bother with it. But it is still a very common cheap and popular substitute for poetry, and critics of literature continue to treat it with a consideration it does not deserve. This is therefore not so much a post-mortem on a dead body as on a body which never was alive at all. But it did impose its spurious imitation of the living reality on a whole generation of poets and their readers, whose ignorance of the real nature of verse concealed from them the impudence of its claim to be either verse or free. Because this ignorance still persists, and because the claims of free verse are not only fraudulent but harmful to real poetry, it seems worth while to examine and expose them.

Free verse, as a movement, is about a hundred years old—it began to influence the poetic tradition with the publication of Walt Whitman's *Leaves of Grass* in 1855. Those who defend free verse sometimes try to give it a more respectable pedigree by pointing to experiments like the choruses in Milton's *Samson Agonistes* or the cadenced prose of Macpherson's *Ossian*. But these were, and remained, literary curiosities which had no perceptible effect on the tradition of English verse. It is interesting to reflect that Whitman too might have remained in the class of literary curiosities but for the transplanting of the idea into French poetry and its replanting in a more virulent form into English poetry somewhat later: a process resembling that by which certain parasites, like the tapeworm and the liver fluke, only become dangerous if they are able to carry out their stages of growth in the bodies of several types of animal in succession.

Whitman himself had no explicit theory of free verse, and the literary storm which raged round *Leaves of Grass* does not seem to have had any serious effect on the practice of

English poetry in the nineteenth century. It was in France at the end of the nineteenth century that what seemed an amusing but harmless eccentricity took root and there incubated a variant form capable of re-infecting English poetry and causing a destructive epidemic. The carriers of the disease in this case appear to have been two expatriate Americans who became French poets: Francis Vielé-Griffin and Stuart Merrill. With Gustave Kahn and Laforgue, they helped to develop a new and virulent form of the free-verse theory among the decadent symbolists of the turn of the century. It remained for two other American expatriates, T. S. Eliot and Ezra Pound, to catch the new form of the infection and transplant it, together with the decayed matrix of symbolist technique and theory, back to England. In 1912 Pound began its spread in England with the first Imagist anthology. From England, mainly by way of Marion Moore's journal *Poetry*, published in Chicago, it spread back to America, where it developed to plague proportions, and, like the great influenza epidemics of the period, spread to almost every country in the world. For a time it became part of the 'Modern Movement' in poetry and a hall-mark of the intellectual and progressive poet as opposed to the academic and traditional versifier.

In the last ten years, however, its vogue has suddenly gone. It is no longer smart and progressive to write in free verse, and those who continue to use it now look a little shabby and old-fashioned to a new generation of poets, and to readers with their own ways of being up-to-date and in the swim.

In the nineteenth century, free verse was often a kind of political gesture. Poets of the left cast off their chains of metre as part of their repudiation of the tyranny of the old régime. Whitman himself seems to have thought of his verse in this way. It was a return to natural, democratic expression, to something more primitive and elemental. The free verse of Whitman was, as he described it himself with some complacency, a 'barbaric yawp', and that was how it struck his contemporaries. It was a challenge to traditional forms of verse, but not a very serious one. You might prefer a barbaric yawp to the eloquence of the Muses, but at least you were not likely to confuse one with the other. So it turned out that the position of traditional poetry was secure enough from assault from without. But the form the theory took among the symbolists was much more insidious, and therefore more dangerous. We find Gustave Kahn in the preface to *Premiers Poèmes* in 1897 arguing that free verse is not an alternative to regular forms but simply a more subtle and developed extension of them. It is the regular forms which are crude, primitive, and limited, and the alexandrine is perfected by free verse, not destroyed by it. The free-verse poets are doing no more than the romantic poets did when they too 'modified' the classical French alexandrine. The evolution of poetry has proceeded step by step from a period when all poets were bound by the same rhythms to the same impersonal expression, and great poets like Corneille or Racine only produced individual master-pieces in spite of the poor and primitive techniques at their disposal. It has now reached a perfection in which each poet has at his disposal a personal and private rhythm for the exact expression of his individual lyric gift.

It was this specious argument which was carried over into the Imagist profession of faith; the second article of this creed was:

> To create new rhythms—as the expression of new moods— and not to copy old rhythms, which merely echo old moods. We do not insist upon 'free verse' as the only method of writing poetry. We fight for it as a principle of liberty. We believe that the individuality of the poet may often be better expressed in free verse than in conventional forms.

The new free verse, therefore, tended to be esoteric and delicate, seeking for nuances of cadence and rhythms expressive of exquisite velleities of feeling. Whitman's 'barbaric yawp' was replaced by Hilda Doolittle's tender phrasing of a momentary impression captured in a cool, detached image. The democratic rhetoric of *Leaves of Grass* had given way to the coy, allusive, intellectual mannerisms of *The Waste Land*. And this corruption of the garrison from within succeeded where the barbarian assault from without had failed. The snob-appeal of the new free verse was effective where the democratic intransigence of the old had made no headway. In order to answer the claims of free verse it is therefore necessary to refute two arguments: one, that free verse replaces a worn-out, artificial and obstructive prosody with something better, more natural and more spontaneous; the other, that free verse is simply the final evolution and perfection of principles of rhythm inherent in the older prosody which was ignorant of the full resources of the language. It is necessary to answer the arguments both for what the French call *vers libre* and also for what they call *vers libéré*.

The starting point for both answers is an understanding of the real nature of the rhythms of traditional verse. Whether the argument against traditional verse-forms is that they are so effete and exhausted that no new effects are possible, or that they are too primitive, coarse, and thumping to express the individual rhythms of a modern sensibility, the fallacy in each case is the same. It consists primarily in a confusion of rhythm and metre. The elements of rhythm in most languages are the same, they consist in alternations of various kinds. The alternations of sound and silence are the simplest and most basic, so that the pauses in continuous speech, such as those we mark by punctuation, form a natural irregular rhythm. Then the alternation of stressed and unstressed or lightly stressed syllables forms another natural rhythm, and as these form themselves into groups, corresponding to the sense, or prose feet, of a wide variety of forms, the rhythm of varying stress imposed upon the rhythm of alternating sound and silence can form extremely rich and varied patterns. Then there is a rhythm formed by the alternation of long and short syllables and another formed by the alternation of the different degrees of pitch that each particular language distinguishes. Finally there is an extremely complex rhythm formed by the alternation and recurrence of sounds of various quality (what sometimes is called verbal

41

music) and in its more deliberately contrived effects it is familiar to us as assonance, alliteration, and rhyme. The rhythmical pattern of even the most clumsy piece of prose or the most incoherent speech is therefore extremely complex. But it need not be pleasing or rich. We distinguish nervous, lively, interesting speech or prose by the degree to which it organizes and orders its rhythms. By the use of certain repeated types of cadence, as in liturgical prose or the so-called verse of Walt Whitman, prose can even be given a principle of recurrence or expectation, but in general the rhythms of prose are subordinated to the semantic pattern of thought. It is the structure of the sentence that determines their rhythms.

Verse employs another set of rhythmic devices in addition to the natural rhythms already described. We call this metre, or measure. The essence of metre is that it is an organization of rhythm on a basis of recurrence or expectation. The alternation of stressed and unstressed syllables occurs in a regular pattern in English—other languages, such as Latin, use an alternation of long and short syllables, and some, such as classical Arabic, have metrical stress and metrical quantity.

The problem of writing verse is that the poet is not faced with a simple choice between regular and irregular rhythms; he must have them all, for they are all part of the language he writes. He cannot change the natural prose-stresses of words or their groupings. He has therefore to fit one set of rhythms into the other so that the expectation of a regularly recurring stress-pattern is satisfied and yet the natural structure of the language is preserved. When we actually read poetry, hearing it instead of mechanically scanning it, we assemble the words into their natural groups according to the sense, the rhythms they would have in prose. We do not read:

Shall *I*.com*pare*.thee *to*.a *sum*.mer's *day*

which is the pattern of the metre, iambic pentameter: what we read is more likely to be:

Shall I.com*pare* thee.to a *sum*mer's.day

which is the prose-grouping of the words according to their

sense. Yet we hear the metrical pattern *through* these prose rhythms. One is, so to speak, counterpointed against the other and the rich and enchanting harmonies of the best poetry are due to this interplay of two sorts of rhythm. The job of a competent poet is to see that the prose and the metrical groupings harmonize and preserve an essential tension and distinctness. If the two coincide too much it will produce a monotonous, unpleasantly sing-song effect, as there will be nothing to give variety to the uniform metrical pattern. If they do not coincide enough, the verse will be either flat and lifeless or halting and clumsy. The variety, music, and colour, the effect of natural ease within a disciplined movement, the heightened tension and elastic force that we associate with poetry, are almost entirely due to the skill with which the two sorts of rhythm are fused in one delightful effect.

It is obvious that two of the claims of free verse must fall immediately to the ground. In the first place its claim to be richer and more free and various in its rhythms compared with the simple jog-trot of metre is seen to be a delusion. The metrical form includes the prose rhythms on which free verse alone depends. And free verse sacrifices at a blow the principal means of heightened tension and richness of texture which arise from the interweaving of one type of rhythm with the other; the whole orchestration of these harmonies is sacrificed to the comparatively tame manipulation of prose rhythms at one level only. To an ear attuned to poetry, the effect of free verse is rather like that of trying to get the same pleasure from dancing when the orchestra has left the ballroom and when the dancers have to improvise their steps as they go along—it may have its moments, but on the whole it is bound to be a dreary and shuffling affair. In the second place it is clear that the main argument against the regular forms: that their possibilities are soon exhausted and the poets in time are reduced to stereotype effect, is absurd. The principles of variation within the iambic pentameter line can be calculated, and they provide inexhaustible variety. Any foot can be replaced by a trochee or a spondee; the caesura may occur after any syllable in the line; more than one substitute foot or more than one caesural pause may occur in various combinations; any line may be end-stopped or run on. When one calculates the number of possible combinations of these varieties of the metrical form with the different possible prose rhythms, rhythms of length, pitch and vowel, and consonantal quality, the varying speeds and effects produced by different combinations of short and polysyllabic words, the mathematical estimate of the possible number of rhythms for a single iambic pentameter line will run into hundreds of thousands. But the single line is itself only a unit in the building up of richer and more complex rhythmic effects each with its balance of regular against 'natural' rhythmical forms. One could point to the almost infinite range of sentence rhythms within the same stanza-forms themselves. Once again the effects and resources on which prose rhythms depend at the level of period, paragraph and chapter, the rhythms of massive structure, are inherent in the structure of regular poetry, and form only one part of its resources.

What then becomes of the attempt of free verse to rival the effects of poetry while confining itself to the resources of prose? The effects of poetry are not mysterious, though they may not be capable of minute analysis or reduction to formulas. If they produce an effect of greater tension, a higher excitement, and a richer texture and harmony, it is because poetry is different in structure from prose, and it is therefore foolish to expect the more limited and different resources of prose to produce these effects. I have already pointed out what these extra resources are. The immense resources of variety within regular verse come from the basic expectation of a regular pattern, which, constantly varying, never disappoints that expectation of regular points of return within the line, of rhyme, of alternation of line with line in the stanza. It is this which gives good poetry its tension, its elasticity, its feeling of grace and vigour, of purposeful and delightful movement. But in free verse there is no point of departure and of return. Each variation in rhythm is simply a variation from that of the last rhythmic group, and where all is variety the end is bound to be monotony. The tolerable free-verse poems, in fact, are all short.

The truth about free verse is that it is not free and it is not verse. It is not free because it has no discipline by which its freedom may be assessed. It is not verse because it has neither measure nor metre. And it is here that the absurdity of *vers libéré* becomes clearer. The effects of all things, natural or contrived, are the results of the sort of things they are; form determines character, and if you change the form you get a different effect. Arrange atoms of carbon in one way and you will get black, greasy graphite; in another way and you will have the hard and brilliant diamond. The material is the same, the form is different. The theory of *vers libéré* is roughly that regular verse passes over into irregular verse by a constant gradation of intermediate forms and that the character of poetry is common to them all. The cruder effects belong to crude repetitive rhythms, and as verse is successfully freed of these it becomes subtler and capable of purer poetic effects. The mistake in this arises from a simple misinterpretation of an historical change that is always going on in poetry, a process by which its life is preserved and renewed.

We have already seen that this life depends on a tension between two sorts of rhythm. Geoffrey Tillotson, in his book on Pope, remarks that 'it seems a law . . . that metre should work by expectation rather than by surprise'. Now surprise comes from variations on the pattern that metre leads us to expect. Without expectation of one thing we cannot be surprised by another, which is why free verse in spite of its variety rarely gives us those shocks of delicious surprise that real poetry always affords. Surprise is dependent on expectation. But it follows from this that there is a natural limit to the amount of variation that any verse-form will bear. After that point is passed the pattern on which expectation is based is lost or so badly damaged that we accept any variation on it without any sense of surprise at all. There is in the variation of any pattern a point of no return, a point at which it ceases to be a definite pattern. On the other hand, in the practice of poets at any period there are always certain variations of the expected pattern which occur so often that they become part of the expectancy and lose their quality of surprise, and poets are driven to find new variations. So there is always a tendency within any verse system towards more and more refinement of effects or towards more and more drastic departure from regular forms.

If you follow the history of a form such as the heroic couplet from Chaucer to Martyn Skinner, for example, you will find a very interesting thing. The expectations are never entirely fixed, they are always being extended or contracted. Certain variations on the expected pattern become, with constant occurrence, part of the expectation. New resources of variety have to be found, and the structure becomes successively loosened and relaxed until in certain passages of Donne's satires there are so many multiple caesuras, run-on lines, inverted and substitute feet that expectation is almost lost. Then the opposite process begins. Waller and Denham begin to restore expectation and reduce variety; the caesura more often falls about the middle of the line, more lines are end-stopped, substitute feet are more tactfully and less plentifully used, until in Pope the optimum of speed, balance and elasticity is reached, to be overpassed in some of Pope's successors; then the pendulum begins to swing the other way. So that each generation of poets sets its successors new problems in metrical pattern to solve—provided that all goes on within the traditional forms. Our age is the first to think it could improve on its predecessors by breaking down the principles of verse altogether and looking for substitute forms. It has been an age which, finding itself at the end of one of those periods of loosening of metrical structure, in its ignorance of the actual anatomy and physiology of verse, imagined that there was no real dividing line between prose and verse at all, and that the effects of one were somehow interchangeable with the other. The confusion was increased by the habit of arbitrary arrangements of the 'lines' of free verse. This meant, as the eye has the natural habit of observing a pause at the end of a line, that what was in fact a passage of prose had imposed on its natural prose rhythms a set of arbitrary, meaningless and usually quite pointless artificial pauses—and it was these which constituted the *verse* of free verse. The truth of this can be tested in practice by printing any piece of *vers libre* as prose. The illusion then disappears and it is almost impossible for anyone who does not know the original line arrangement to restore it. Let us test it without more ado:

> Three white leopards sat under a juniper tree in the cool of the day, having fed to satiety on my legs my heart and my liver and that which had been contained in the hollow round of my skull. And God said: Shall these bones live? Shall these bones live?

That is a plain passage of prose though it comes from a work treated with the greatest reverence as poetry by contemporary critics. The claim of free verse is that it creates rhythms which, unlike the coarse and generalized *rub-a-dub-dub* of regular verse, are the precise expression of an individual and unique mood and nuance of thought. But what is gained or lost by printing this passage from T. S. Eliot's *Ash Wednesday* as follows:

> *Three white leopards*
> *Sat under a juniper tree in the cool of the day,*
> *Having fed to satiety on my legs my heart and my liver*
> *And that which had been contained in the hollow*
> *Round of my skull*
> *And God said: Shall these bones live? Shall*
> *These bones*
> *Live?*

or indeed in any other arbitrary arrangement, including the one actually chosen for it by its author? The poets of half a century or more ago who wrote what they called 'prose poems' were in fact more honest. The prose poem did not pretend to be what it was not. It was prose attempting to reproduce the effects of poetry by using all the ornaments of poetry but not its form. The effect was meretricious and unconvincing, and demonstrated, if demonstration was needed, that the structure of regular verse is something more than a pretty trick. In the same way one has only to look at some examples of so-called *vers libre* to see that for the most part it consists of broken-down iambic pentameter verse, and that, as soon as a point is reached when the pattern of recurrence is lost, the expectation vanishes and what we have at last is prose in an arbitrary line arrangement.

Mr Graham Hough in his Warton Lecture for English Poetry in 1957 admitted that *vers libre* was for the most part merely prose in masquerade. He tried to save the day for *vers libéré*. Discussing some lines from T. S. Eliot's *Prufrock* he shows that for all their irregularity they do contain blank verse: 'they can be read as a perfectly natural development of Jacobean blank verse, handled it is true, very freely, but with the same kind of freedom as that employed by the dramatists we know Mr Eliot to have studied'.

Let us not admit, for the moment, that a great deal of nonsense has been talked about the dramatic verse of Jacobean plays, and that in Mr Eliot's case this nonsense has amounted to special pleading for his own particular prosodic nonsense. Let us see what Mr Hough makes of the lines in question:

The yellow fog that rubs its back upon the window panes
The yellow smoke that rubs its muzzle on the window panes
Licked its tongue into the corner of the evening

He reprints it as follows:

The yellow fog that rubs its back upon
The window-panes, the yellow smoke that rubs
Its muzzle on the window-panes, licked
Its tongue into the corners of the evening

48

'It becomes,' he says, 'perfectly recognizable blank verse, though it is not printed as such.' One can only remark that, while it might have passed as prose, it is about the flattest and most incompetent blank verse one would look to see, and that bad and corrupted verse masquerading as prose is no more likely to be poetry than prose masquerading as verse. *Vers libéré* is in fact verse from which nearly all the vitality, grace, and tension has been removed by breaking down its metrical structure almost to the point where it passes over into prose. A whole generation of poets has followed T. S. Eliot into this waste land of prosody where verse, half dead, trails its flabby rhythms and dispirited cadences across the page, on the plea that the old forms were dead and that this moribund prosody was a means of resurrecting the divine dance of language.

But there is another aspect of the historical process which makes nonsense of the idea that the traditional resources of metre can ever be exhausted or that the old forms can ever be regarded as dead or unusable. Not only do the metrical forms renew themselves as such in the way I have suggested, but the rhythms of poetry, as we saw, depend on an elastic tension and harmony between metrical pattern and prose rhythms. But language changes from generation to generation. Its pitch, its prose rhythms, its pronunciation, are always subtly changing like its vocabulary. One of the delights of reading poetry of the past is to catch the echoes of a living contemporary speech and to see how different are the rhythmical effects it draws from the same metrical devices in different ages. A new poetic style, if it is alive, usually begins from the rhythm of contemporary speech. As the style develops it tends to become fixed until it has become a poetic language, distinguished as a literary dialect from what is by now contemporary speech. Then a new poet of genius restores it by going back to contemporary language once more. What Chaucer, Shakespeare, Donne, Dryden, Wordsworth, Tennyson, and perhaps W. H. Auden have done in their time may be done again. The language itself provides continual new resources for rejuvenating the traditional

49

patterns and providing them with new and yet traditional music. The whole notion that the capital resources of poetry were limited and would one day be exhausted is no more than a bogy based on ignorance of the real nature of language. Not only is the remedy of free verse a bogus remedy, the disease it pretends to cure is a popular delusion.

The Middle Way

THERE are two ways in which a metrical form, like any other artistic style, can fall into decadence. The craftsmen can continue to refine on it until every possible effect and nuance has been mastered, and the sensibility that responds to its perfections may then continue its attempts to refine still further till it convinces itself of effects which are purely imaginary. It believes itself to be discriminating where in fact the differences are so minimal that no distinction is possible. Spurious connoisseurship replaces real judgment. Or else one master brings the style to such perfection that no one ever again manages to match that skill, and the style declines from the mere sense of inept imitation which overtakes all subsequent attempts. This, I believe, is what happened to the heroic couplet in the eighteenth century.

Iambic pentameter verse depends for its ease and flow mainly on two things: the movement of the caesura and the extent to which the sense is allowed to 'run on', syntactically speaking, beyond the limit of the line. In every line there is at least one real or imaginary point of pause. It is a real pause when it marks the end of a phrase or a sentence; an imaginary pause when it is merely the place where you would pause if you had to draw breath or might wait for dramatic effect. This caesural pause may occur after any of the ten syllables in the line.

1st What, // have his daughters brought him to this pass.
2nd Holland, // that scarce deserves the name of land.
3rd The heartache // and the thousand natural ills.
4th A gentle Knight // was pricking on the plain.
5th Keep up your bright swords // for the dew will rust them.
6th Is it not passing brave // to be a king.
7th Fretted the pigmy body // to decay.
8th Is it not brave to be a King, // Techelles.
9th At the round earth's imagined corners // blow.

And of course there can be one, two, three, or four caesural pauses in a line. Part of the curious effect of Donne's elegies and satires is due to his excessive use of inversion and substitution and to hypermetrical effects. But their characteristic movement is due to his constant use of two or three strong caesural pauses, a characteristic also of Gerard Manley Hopkins and to a lesser degree of Ben Jonson.

But the line is only a unit in a larger rhythm. Blank verse is based on the paragraph, other verse on the stanza. The couplet is the minimal form of stanza, but by letting the sense and the syntax run over the limits of the couplet one can achieve very nearly the run-on effect of blank verse. This has been the practice of all good poets from Chaucer on. The end result of the process is to be seen in Donne's satires when he even cuts words in the middle for a rhyme, and the verse though powerful is so crabbed, jerky and awkward that the principle of expectation is almost gone.

> *Graccus loves all as one, and thinks that so*
> *As women do in divers countries goe*
> *In divers habits, yet are still one kinde*
> *So doth, so is Religion; and this blind-*
> *nesse too much light breeds;* (SATIRE III)

It is no wonder that Pope felt that Donne needed 'versifying'. When poets began to feel a need to reform the heroic couplet, what Waller, Denham and Dryden did was to cut down the number of substitute feet, to make the sense pause in a larger number of cases at the end of the line, to keep the couplets more like separate stanzas by closing them more often—that is by making them end with a major syntactic pause, a full stop or a semicolon, so that they were syntactically self-contained—and above all to limit the number of caesuras in the line to one or at most two, and lastly to place them, as Pope recommended, in the majority of cases after the fourth, fifth, or sixth syllable of the line.

The reforms of Dryden, who acknowledged his debt to Waller and Denham (through Sir George Mackenzie, who

first drew his attention to these poets), may be illustrated if
we take the verses of Donne just quoted and rearrange them
on the lines suggested. This is how Waller or Denham might
have rewritten Donne's lines:

> *All, Graccus loves as one and thinks that so*
> *As women are, Religion must be too:·*
> *Women in divers lands wear divers weeds*
> *But too much light, in Graccus, blindness breeds.*

One feels at once the added speed and balance, though
the rewriting has lost, or loses, some of the tortured force
and energy of the original. But it is still comparatively rough
verse. If you turn to almost any passage from Dryden's *Virgil*
your ear should detect the same sort of movement. Dryden,
while preserving the rich variety of the rhythms, had added
to the normal expectation the feeling for closed couplets,
end-stopped lines, and a caesura near the middle of the line
which gave it an effect of balance. Pope refined on these
tendencies. First of all, he increased the balance about the
middle of the line, cut down the number of inversions,
avoided hiatus and hypermetrical effects, and for preference
made the rhyme-word a monosyllable—he avoids feminine
rhymes as much as possible. Then he developed a number
of devices making one half of the line balance, mirror, repeat,
or invert the movement of the other, and one line of the
couplet balance or subtly contrast with the other. The following example of his mature style is taken from the 'Epistle
to Augustus':

> *The laugh, the jest, attendants on the bowl,*
> *Smooth'd ev'ry brow, and open'd ev'ry soul:*
> *With growing years the pleasing Licence grew,*
> *And Taunts alternate innocently flew.*
> *But Times corrupt, and Nature, ill-inclin'd,*
> *Produc'd the point that left a sting behind;*
> *Till friend with friend, and families at strife,*
> *Triumphant Malice rag'd thro' private life.*
> *Who felt the wrong, or fear'd it, took th' alarm,*

THE CAVE AND THE SPRING

Appeal'd to Law, and Justice lent her arm.
At length, by wholesom dread of statutes bound,
The Poets learn'd to please, and not to wound:
Most warp'd to Flatt'ry's side; but some, more nice,
Preserv'd the freedom, and forbore the vice.
Hence Satire rose, that just the medium hit,
And heals with Morals what it hurts with Wit.

This passage contains a good deal of the devices by which Pope maintains at once the illusion of balance so perfect that even good critics have sometimes failed to see that he is always deserting it, and the continuity and variety that poetry demands. The secret is to make us expect lines of the pattern

Preserv'd the freedom, and forbore the vice.

where each part of each half of the line matches the other syntactically and rocks on the centre word as a pivot, and where the sense matches like the syntax. But while he constantly returns to this tightest form of the pattern he realizes that it would be intolerably artificial if kept up just like that. So he has an almost inexhaustible number of equivalents; for example:

The laugh, the jest, // attendants on the bowl,

where the balance is one of meaning and the rhythm is quite different in the two halves.

Smooth'd ev'ry brow, and open'd ev'ry soul:

is the basic pattern, but with a subtle contrast of sense: *allaying* versus *arousing.*

With growing years // the pleasing Licence grew,

The balance is between the two participial phrases and the pivot word comes at the end instead of in the middle.

And Taunts alternate // innocently flew.

balances noun-adjective, in reversed order, against adverb-verb also in reversed order.

But Times corrupt, and Nature, ill-inclin'd,

balances corrupting Time against unfriendly Nature, but

loosens the tight rhythmic structure by a double caesura and then tightens it again in the second half of the couplet:

> *Produc'd the point that left a sting behind;*

These are only a few of the variants. Pope keeps up the balanced tension but produces the effect of ease and variety by innumerable variations of the same basic device. In the same way, without running over from couplet to couplet, yet, by continuous logical development of the train of thought from each couplet to the next and by skilful use of linking words, he keeps them from splitting up into separate epigrams. In the eight couplets I have quoted, four begin with such words as *But, Till, At length, Hence.*

Now we can guess at how Pope might have revised the lines from Donne. At the Denham-Waller-Dryden level I suggested they might stand thus:

> *All Graccus loves as one and thinks that so*
> *As women are, Religion must be too:*
> *Women in divers lands wear divers weeds*
> *But too much light, in Graccus, blindness breeds.*

I suggest that Pope might have tightened this up as follows:

> *As Turks in every clime adore the fair*
> *Deaf to their tongues and blind to what they wear,*
> *The light of faith in Saul a blindness breeds*
> *To love the churches but ignore the creeds.*

Pope would probably not have passed those lines. They represent more nearly what happened to the poets who learned the obvious tricks from Pope but never mastered the delicate ear for the varying tension of words, the stresses and resolutions that occur where the rhythm and the sense interact in such a way that you cannot extricate what each contributes. They lack his harmony and clarity and, because they lack the skilful modulation by which each line in Pope is planned and adjusted to those that precede and follow, they stand each alone in a sort of wooden isolation. Pope's control became so absolute in the end that he did what no

E

one else could do with the heroic couplet: he relaxed his own rules, varied the place of the caesura at will, used inversion and substitution freely, used run-on lines and feminine rhymes, and all without changing the speed, ease, clarity and apparent tension and balance. The Third Book of *The Dunciad* is particularly interesting in this respect. Here one sees Pope as it were playing with his skill: breaking measure only to resolve the discord so skilfully that harmony seems not only preserved but enhanced. Observe the placing of the caesuras in

> *Lo! Rome herself, proud mistress now no more*
> *Of arts, but thundering against heathen lore.*

One might find it hard to match that in the early poems. A few lines further on we read

> *Behold yon isle, by Palmers, Pilgrims trod*
> *Men, bearded, bald, cowl'd, uncowl'd, shod, unshod,*
> *Peel'd, patch'd and pyebald, linsey wolsey brothers*
> *Grave Mummers! sleeveless some, and shirtless others*
> *That once was Britain!*

Taken out of their context these lines are surprising, but in the context they are perfectly resolved by the return to the 'strong pattern' that follows.

The later eighteenth century as represented by even as good a poet as Cowper shows how all the obvious tricks of Pope's style could easily be copied. The secret of the internal tension that makes his lines vibrate and glow was never caught again.

I have found this in trying to imitate him. Time and again I thought I had caught the secret, but after a few days when I looked at my verses they seemed comparatively wooden and quite lacked the marvellous animation and elastic tension of the master's.

The fact is that we have largely lost the ear for the fine effects of this sort of verse. It is obvious that Pope and Johnson in their criticism are often making discriminations of importance which are difficult for us to follow, and that they were responsive to felicities which we miss, or which we confound with effects they would have regarded as comparatively crude or trite. More than any other poetry, perhaps, the eighteenth-century heroic couplets require connoisseurship—the sort of educated discrimination that people think worth acquiring in the world of wine and which was at one time the natural attitude to poetry. It requires a highly trained and disciplined taste, and involves perhaps some narrowing of sympathy, though not necessarily so. Since the end of the eighteenth century the 'natural' attitude to poetry has been to widen sympathies, to enjoy broad effects, and there has been a consequent dulling of the keen edge, of that educated discrimination which the eighteenth century could assume in its readers.

This discriminating taste is the basis of the much misunderstood idea of 'correctness' in poetry, the correctness which Pope in early youth made it his aim to bring to the practice of English verse, and which his *Essay on Criticism* is meant both to explain and to exemplify. Correctness is not primarily a matter of following explicit and ideal 'rules' of versification but of exercising discrimination in choices that tremble on the very limit of sensibility. Far from being a mechanical skill, it is one that depends on continual acts of judgment so little referable to any rule of thumb that they may look arbitrary to those who do not share the writer's discipline of taste. Correctness is the mastery of all that is implied in Horace's doctrine of the middle way.

This doctrine is extremely important. In the first place it means of course avoidance of excess, it means common sense and urbanity, the great ideals of eighteenth-century literature; but it means much more than this because Horace does not mean that art should be mediocre. It is actually a counsel of perfection and its following makes poetry the difficult and exacting art it is. If we try to conceive the standard we shall perhaps get nearest to it by thinking of aiming at a target or tuning a musical instrument. Excess means being wide of the mark, of course—there is only one bull's-eye and it can only be hit by exact aiming; there is only one pitch which will put the instrument exactly in tune. Anything a little to one side or the other will be a miss and a miss is as good as a mile. It is no good having your instrument nearly in tune. It must be exactly in tune or it may as well be quite out. This is the concept or something like the concept of the middle path, which is not mediocrity but perfection. What is true of tuning the instrument is true also of playing it. There is only one perfect execution of the music and it demands the greatest skill to arrive at it. Most of the executants will approach this perfect norm, but fail to reach it, some too loud, some a little too flat, some a little mechanical, some too emotional, and so on. This is mediocrity. Beyond this are the various forms of excess into which the player may be driven if instead of aiming at the perfection he aims at avoiding some other excess. This is the commonest of faults, because it is easier to see what glaring faults consist in than to see what excellence consists in. Moreover, what is true of the execution of the music is true of the composition. Here too perfection consists of a sort of mean which is just right and which just to miss lands you in mediocrity.

The doctrine of the middle way implies another: the doctrine of *no second best*. In this, art differs from other human pursuits. 'A second-rate lawyer or pleader', says Horace, 'has not the excellence of Messala's eloquence or the legal knowledge of Aulus Cascellius, yet he has his value. To poets to be second-rate is a privilege which neither men nor gods nor bookstalls ever allowed.' There is on this theory no such thing as moderately good poetry any more than there can be a moderately tuned note. It is either in tune or out of tune. Of course this does not mean that good poems will be faultless, especially long ones. Even Homer will nod. Even the best player will occasionally produce a wrong note. This is a different thing however from the extravagance or the mediocrity which are simply *bad*.

This is a most important and interesting doctrine and it is the real basis of the neo-classic notion of correctness. Looked at from this point of view, correctness is not a mere finicky concern with *not* breaking rules or with observing minutiae of good form, it is not merely a matter of elegance and urbanity, it is the principle of beauty itself.

This leads us to the next Horatian canon, that of plainness and clarity and order. This beauty is achieved by hitting the exquisite mean. It can only be achieved, in fact it only has any meaning, in a world of order and precision and limits. Beauty is not only the limit at which you aim, it is the *only* limit, because the further you proceed in any direction from this the further you go into the disorderly, the extravagant, and there is no limit in any direction. There is a limited number of notes in the musical scale and their relationship is exact (to return to the metaphor I have been using to clarify what Horace is saying), but the number of possible intermediate or untuned notes and discords is infinite and they have no perceptible order. Beauty is not only exactness but order and limit. A large part of Horace's epistle is concerned with the way every part of a work should be consonant with the whole, or deals with the various types of bad writing which do not possess this clarity, order and perspicuity. He warns young Piso against introducing purple patches which are out of place simply in order to brighten a dull passage or to surprise or excite the reader. Everything that goes into the work must be consonant with the whole. A poem should be something 'simplex et unum', simple and unified. The point of 'simplex' as far as I can see is *not* that Horace is demanding no *complexity* but that he is against over-elaboration. A poem must not only be an actual unity but it must be simple enough for us to comprehend it as a unity. If it exceeds what we can take in as a unity, then it might as well be chaotic.

From all these we can arrive at the doctrine of style. Obviously the style which will suit these demands of beauty best will be one which has no extravagances; it will be plain, clear and exact and it will by exactness and by the clarity and order of the whole treatment achieve a miraculous rightness which is beauty. Such writing will have a deceptive appearance of natural, effortless ease, almost ordinary in its apparent lack of effort. But it is the perfection which comes only from endless effort joined with genius. Those who try to copy it will only imitate its superficial character and will end in mediocrity. 'My aim shall be a poem,' says Horace, 'so moulded of common materials that all the world may hope as much for itself, may toil hard, and yet toil in vain if it attempts as much, such is the potency of order and arrangement, with such dignity may things of common life be clothed.'

Now this is what Pope actually achieved in poetry and it is the principle for which he and Swift fought all their lives. This is what lies behind the *Battle of the Books* of Swift and Pope's *Dunciad*. This is the fundamental concept of classicism, the root of its aesthetic.

The Horatian ideal, of course, easily degenerates into mere urbanity where genius and passion are wanting. It easily becomes writing to a frigid and mechanical formula since it tends always to *narrow down the technique*. And this is what happened to poetry in the latter part of the eighteenth century with writers who lacked the passion of Pope and for whom the heroic couplet had become merely a knife-edge or tightrope on which they had to walk.

The Satiric Muse

THE title indicates the problem, for there is, in fact, no acknowledged muse of satire. Epic poetry, lyric poetry, comedy, tragedy, and sacred poetry, dancing and singing, which are only connected with poetry, all have their presiding muses and so have history and astronomy, which have long ceased to be associated with a poetic form, but not satire, which is one of the great departments of the art. Satire in fact has always been regarded with suspicion. Even in the middle of the eighteenth century, when it was the dominant form of poetry and enjoyed a prestige that it never had before or since, we find Joseph Warton, in his famous essay on the 'Genius and Writings of Pope', denying that Pope was a poet of the highest order since he lacked 'the pathetick and the sublime', a view echoed a century later by Matthew Arnold when he denied to the poetry of Dryden and Pope passion and high seriousness. By Arnold's day indeed satire had fallen into disrepute and decay as a form of poetry. Neither the nineteenth-century nor the twentieth-century poets have practised it much and it has come to be classed with comic and occasional verse.

Pope, our finest master of verse satire, did not agree that satire was incapable of either passion or sublimity. In the *Epilogue to the Satires* there is a magnificent passage in which Pope in some of the most passionate verse in the language defends the high seriousness of the form. The friend with whom the poem shows him conversing has accused him of pride in presuming to set up as the judge of private folly and public vice, and the poet replies

> So proud, I am no Slave:
> So impudent, I own myself no Knave:
> So odd, my Country's Ruin makes me grave.
> Yes, I am proud; I must be proud to see
> Men not afraid of God, afraid of me:

Safe from the Bar, the Pulpit, and the Throne,
Yet touch'd and sham'd by Ridicule *alone.*
  O sacred Weapon! left for Truth's defence,
Sole Dread of Folly, Vice, and Insolence!
To all but Heav'n-directed hands deny'd,
The Muse may give thee, but the Gods must guide.

These are high claims. Satire as the voice of public opinion
has a social function that places it on a level with Religion,
Law, and Government. Though its tone may be light, its
function is wholly serious; and as for passion, it is actuated
by a fierce and strenuous moral and intellectual enthusiasm,
the passion for order, justice, and beauty.

Yet I have always found it difficult to persuade my students
to take satire seriously as poetry. They resist the notion that
the *Epilogue to the Satires* could be poetry just as intense, as
deeply evocative of feeling, as instinct with beauty as, say,
Keats's *Ode to a Nightingale.* They can be led quite easily
to enjoy good satire, its wit, its farce, its ridicule, its invec-
tive, its serious intention. But ask them to discuss it as *poetry*
and they find it lacking precisely in the feeling they associate
with poetry. I used to think that perhaps they had been
badly taught at school, but this is not the case. In fact few
of them had any acquaintance with verse satire before they
came to the university. The causes lie deeper, and in some
years of teaching I have managed, I think, to unravel some
of them.

There is first of all a general suspicion of what I may call
Applied Poetry in distinction from *Pure Poetry.* Satire is
poetry written with a definite social purpose. It is unasham-
edly and openly didactic. It is plain propaganda. Now for
the last hundred years, ever since the aesthetic movement
began, it has been taken almost as a self-evident truth that
the highest art is pure art, that is to say, it has no purpose
outside itself. It is justified simply in being what it is,
aesthetic structure designed for aesthetic enjoyment, a doctrine summed up rather ambiguously in the well-known
phrase: Art for Art's sake! The doctrine may be rather dis-
credited today, but the general attitude of mind that it pro-

moted still persists. It is an attitude reinforced by a belief expressed by Edgar Allan Poe in a famous essay, that there is one pure essence of poetry, which is to be found in the short lyric of intense feeling. This led him to deny that description, reasoning, narration were things that differentiated one *kind* of poetry from another. There are not, he thought, different species of poetry at all, but only one sort of pure poetry, unnecessarily diluted by telling stories, arguing cases or describing people and scenery. The belief in pure poetry has also become something of a dogma in our time and on both counts satire would obviously rank low, for it attempts to reform and warn and it is diluted with description, argument, and narrative.

Satire has probably less claim to be pure poetry than any other poetic form, though Pope in the introduction to *The Dunciad* made a delightful, and not very serious plea for it on these grounds. In the eighteenth century there was a number of attempts to demonstrate the existence and the goodness of God from the evidence of creation. The existence of God could be inferred from the fact that there appeared to be a rational design in the whole system of Nature, and this argued an intelligent creator of the world; the goodness of God could be inferred from asking ourselves what purpose was served by any created being. Sheep had obviously been provided to give wool for clothes; even vermin had a purpose, for they encourage us to keep clean. The world is full of fools. What possible purpose in the Great Design can such a quantity of fools serve. Pope makes the monstrous suggestion that as fools serve no purpose in themselves, Providence has created them as raw material for satire. 'For whoever will consider the Unity of the whole design, will be sensible, that the *Poem* was not made for these Authors, but these Authors for the *Poem*.' Satire looked at in this way is not primarily applied poetry at all. It is pure poetry creating beautiful and amusing works of art from the natural material which the goodness of God has so kindly supplied to his poets. Absurd as the idea is, it contains an important truth. A poem is a poem not in virtue of what it sets out to do but in virtue of what it is. *Paradise Lost* sets out to justify the ways of God to man. Its purpose is theological and didactic. You may think its theology unsound and its argument ineffective. But it is still a magnificent *poem*. Satire in verse is primarily poetry. It is to be judged by its beauty and effectiveness as poetry in the first instance and only secondarily by its effectiveness as social or moral propaganda. The curious thing is that we often fail to recognize this in the case of satire whereas we accept it as a matter of course in the case of religious poetry. The reason for this is not hard to see. *Paradise Lost* has what Matthew Arnold called 'high seriousness' both morally and poetically. That is to say the emotions *in* the poem, religious awe, reverence, tragic pity, and moral concern, are matched by the emotion *of* the poem, sublime poetic fervour, whereas with satire the emotion *in* the poem may vary from a feeling of the grotesque and absurd to real anger and violent hatred, and this obscures the emotion *of* the poem, which is one of enjoyment and celebration.

This confusion of the emotion that a work of art embodies in its treatment of its subject with the emotion produced by the work as a work of art, is a common one and is one of the bugbears of criticism. A famous painting of Goya's depicts the massacres that followed a popular uprising in Madrid during the Napoleonic wars. Goya, it is said, stood at his window and watched the executions that went on all night and, in deep horror and indignation, painted the picture that records them. Men and women, lined up against a wall by torchlight, face a French firing squad. Before them lie the mutilated bodies of the previous batch of victims. Every detail of fear, despair and defiance is strikingly caught. It is impossible to describe the horror of the scene. That is the emotion *in* the picture. But the picture itself is a masterpiece of design, colour and detail. The beauty of the picture as a picture is itself an element in the horror of the subject, but it is something more: it is a triumphant assertion of the artistic vision; the emotion of the picture, as opposed to the emotion *in* the picture, is one of radiance and joy.

Much the same distinction can be made in the case of satire. When Pope lashes Lord Hervey in the character of Sporus the emotion in the poem is one of ferocious contempt, disgust and, one must admit, some personal malice— Pope simply could not feel detached about Hervey—but the attack is couched in verse of such exquisite beauty, in language so pure, economical, and exact, that its effect is like that of triumphant music. Its gaiety, its irrepressible spontaneity, its grace and certainty make it one of the finest passages of pure poetry in the language. When Dryden attacks the gross and stupid poet Shadwell in *Mac Flecknoe* he does so in terms which create the emotion that accompanies contemptuous abuse. When the absurd old poetaster Flecknoe chooses Shadwell as his heir, he says

> *'t is resolved; for Nature pleads that he*
> *Should only rule who most resembles me:*
> *Shadwell alone my perfect image bears,*
> *Mature in dullness from his tender years;*
> *Shadwell alone of all my sons is he*
> *Who stands confirmed in full stupidity*
> *The rest to some faint meaning make pretence*
> *But Shadwell never deviates into sense!*

The rising excitement of the three triumphant statements has the feeling of a fanfare of trumpets to which Dryden's real dislike and contempt for Shadwell is only a sort of accompaniment. The emotion of the sentiments expressed is personal and particular; the emotion of the poetry is universal and detached. It is because it is easy to feel that in the *Ode to a Nightingale* the subject and the poetry are in harmony, that we find it harder to give the Satiric Muse her due where the subject and the poetry are nearly always at variance. They are at variance of course, but they do not conflict, for the poetry is almost always asserting those values which the attack is also concerned to assert.

Another common objection to satire is that it commonly claims to wage war on vice, folly, bad taste, and stupidity. The metaphor of warfare is perhaps unfortunate, for wars are usually lost or won, and vice, folly and stupidity are neither beaten nor abolished by the wars that satire wages. This has led some people to doubt the sincerity of satire. Either the poet is a fool if he believes that poetry, however angry, however effective as mockery, can really make fools less foolish or vicious men less vicious—or else the poet is really using a pretence of high-minded purpose as a cloak for abusing people he does not like and his real motive is personal malice. Personal malice is not a very admirable passion, and malice cloaked in hypocrisy is downright disgusting.

But of course this is seriously to misunderstand the aim of the satirist. Pope makes this clear when he equates the function of satire with those of the bar, the pulpit, and the throne. All have the same function of maintaining the order and integrity of society. The church does not hope to eradicate wickedness and impiety. Sin is original in man and will always recur. But if it cannot be eradicated, it can and must be kept in check; the law does not hope to eradicate crime, it exists to keep it within bounds and to deter criminals by the fear of efficient detection and appropriate punishment. The administrators of the state do not hope to make corruption in public life impossible, yet if the leaders of the nation do their job they can hope to make an example of corrupt officials and to make the venal afraid to take bribes or use power unjustly because they know the risk and fear it. The claim of satire is much the same. It keeps the public conscience alert, it exposes absurdity for what it is and makes those who are inclined to adopt foolish or tasteless fashions aware that they are ridiculous. It shows vice its own feature and makes it odious to others. If you have a garden you do not hope to eradicate weeds for ever. But if you stop weeding your beds you will soon have no garden at all. This is the sense in which satire wages war. It is a war that can never end in a complete victory, but, in a sense, if the campaign is well conducted its victory is a continuous one.

But I suspect that what makes poets avoid the Satiric Muse in this age is not chiefly a feeling that satire cannot be poetry or that it cannot be effective. It is rather a disinclination to set up as a judge of morals, manners or taste. Satire is an aristocratic art. It is not afraid to tell unpopular truths, but its habit is to tell them with the assurance and detachment of ridicule, and ridicule is the weapon of contempt.

Imagine a poet today who in the spirit of Pope or of Dryden felt called on to deride the processes of commercial advertising. Anyone of the slightest taste, common sense, or regard for truth has only to spend a single day listening to commercial radio or television—if he can stand it—and to reflect that most of our people listen to it *by preference* in all their leisure hours, to find himself appalled and delighted at the same time. The absurdity of its monstrous pretensions lends itself to comedy. The irony of seeing the resources of science, the great achievements of human genius ending in this sort of application is the very basis of intellectual satire. The picture of systematic degradation of public taste, the slow and persistent perversion of judgment, the steady operation of moronic intelligence to produce a world safe and profitable for morons, must arouse in the satirist that *saeva indignatio* which animated Swift. If he reflects that a number of these stations are owned and run by the churches who are supposed to discourage systematic lying for gain, he will perceive the operation of that psychological Gresham's Law by which bad money drives out good. His satire would in fact have the same basis as Pope's *Dunciad*. What would happen if he attacked one of the most powerful forms of business in such a way that he named names and was really effective, I leave you to imagine. But this needs only a little courage and it can be done. What is more likely to deter a poet is an obscure feeling that he should not set himself up as a man with superior intellectual standards, superior taste or morals to his fellow men, to tell them that nine-tenths of them have minds that prefer garbage and to make fun of them at their grisly troughs. So the poets leave this to the caricaturist, the novelist, the *diseur* and the dramatist, who in our age have given the Satiric Muse a home.

The Sincerity of Poetry

SOME time ago I took part in a television interview in which the interviewer asked the surprising question: Why are you obsessed with sex? When I asked what made her ask that she said it was because so many of my poems were concerned with sex, and she was not to be moved from this point of view by my reply that on the contrary I thought they were concerned with love. Nor was she convinced by my pointing out that there were nearly as many references to birds and to religion in the poems in question and that nobody on these grounds had ever accused me of an ornithological obsession or of a tendency to religious mania.

It is plain that there is a curious and irrational difference between the arts in this respect. A novelist or a dramatist may concern himself almost entirely with the relations between the sexes and nobody will think him obsessed or perverse if he takes this as his material and deals with it minutely and realistically. There seems to be some vague public sentiment about poets which feels they ought to operate on a more ethereal plane. If a novelist insists on putting his characters into bed and telling us what happened there, there may be some protests but they will be protests that indicate that this is no more than what is to be expected of writers of fiction. But if a poet does the same thing the protests will suggest that he is going outside the proper field of poetry. A painter may spend most of his working life painting naked women in every possible seductive attitude, and the critics will only talk about his masterly flesh tints, his management of the masses and the rhythms of his composition. But let a poet describe a lady with all her clothes off with an attention to details such as the painter would think himself obliged to give the subject and the critics will talk about him as though he were Peeping Tom.

It is only, I suppose, that poets suffer a little more at the

68

hands of that ingrained puritanism of the Western mind, which even in this age regards all the arts as morally danger- ous unless kept to innocuous subjects or compelled to ob- serve certain deep-rooted taboos. In a famous and eloquent passage from *The Idea of a University*, Cardinal Newman, defending secular literature as a university study, called literature 'the life and remains of the natural man', and he argued that no serious study of literature could go on unless one was prepared to study the whole subject even though, as he put it, the old Adam smelt rank in it. It would be absurd in the study of medicine to leave out certain organs and functions of the body on the ground of modesty, and literature is no less serious a study than medicine. But a serious study demands a serious treatment, and a complete treatment to provide the materials of the whole study. The writer's approach to the subject is not necessarily either clinical or scientific, but there is a sense in which, like the scientist, he wants to tell the truth and the whole truth about the world of man. The poet who attempts to do so is likely to find that however serious his approach, however important the things he has to say, he is refused the freedom allowed, not only to the doctor or the psychologist, but even to the historian and the anthropologist. What in the others is granted to be an inquiring mind, in the field of literature is apt to be labelled a dirty mind.

What seems peculiar to poetry among other arts is the constant tendency to take poems as confessions, to regard them as parts of the poet's autobiography. This is particu- larly the case perhaps with poems that deal with sexual love. The reader will be sure to take them, if not as confessions, at least as translations of personal experience. A poem that pictured a hungry man thinking of a superb dinner course by course, or even bite by bite, would not lead us to think that the poet was starving when he wrote. But a poem which deals not merely with the feelings of the lover, but with the act and ceremonies of making love will almost automatically brand him as obsessed with sexual desire. It is hard for most readers to distinguish the poem from the poet, no matter what his subject may be. What the poem says is apt to be taken by general readers and professional critics alike for what the poet thinks or feels. In other forms of literature, in drama and fiction, for example, readers have learned to distinguish the author's own attitude from opinions and ideas expressed through the characters or even put forward as part of the dramatic setting.

To take an example: Joseph Furphy's *Such is Life* is full of opinions of the supposed author Tom Collins, but critics have learned to distinguish between Tom Collins and Joseph Furphy, even though many of the views and opinions are in fact those of Furphy himself. In the novel Furphy creates another self, the hero of the book, who so to speak acts out some of his own views but with a difference that is important. Now, except with dramatic poetry, this is something that readers and critics of poetry hardly ever manage to do. In the ordinary non-dramatic poem the poet is nearly always taken to be expressing his personal views, feelings and attitudes. One cannot entirely blame critics, of course, since this is precisely what a lot of poets try to do. It is an attitude to poetry characteristic of a great many poets since the so-called romantic revival at the end of the eighteenth century. The prevailing view of poetry since then has been influenced by such theories as that which holds poetry to be the overflow or expression of powerful feelings, or that which holds that poetry is an expression of the poet's personality. It was against this prevailing view that T. S. Eliot protested more than fifty years ago. Poetry, he said, requires not the expression but the sacrifice of personality, the surrender of the poet's self to something which is more valuable. The emotion a poem creates is not the emotion that produced it. It may look like the expression of a personal feeling. The poet may even appear to be speaking in the first person, but the emotion in the poem is not even then to be taken as a personal emotion.

My meaning is, that the poet has, not a 'personality' to express, but a particular medium, which is only a medium and not a personality, in which impressions and experiences combine in peculiar and unexpected ways. Impressions and experiences which are important for the man may take no place in the poetry, and those which become important in the poetry may play quite a negligible part in the man, the personality...

This is a view to which I would thoroughly subscribe though it may not be equally true for all poets. When I set out to write a poem I have a general idea of the way I want it to go but in the process of writing it I find that it insists on going a different way. Though I am sometimes prepared to subscribe to feelings or attitudes of mind which poems express, after I have written them, these are often different from what I would regard as my permanent attitudes and feelings. I rarely read reviews of my work but when I do I am sometimes surprised when critics attribute to me views which I would contend belong not to me but to the poems.

If I am surprised, and sometimes irritated, it is not, I think, a matter of any importance. But it does lead me to reflect on what the sincerity of poetry consists in. If we are deeply moved by a poem, we like to think that the writer meant it to be moving, and that the art of poetry is not simply a trick which can impose factitious emotions as genuine. And we are right in thinking so. But this does not justify us in supposing that what a poem says or leads us to feel is what its author must think or feel. Sincerity in the arts is not to be tested as simply as this. Poetry must be communicated but it is not primarily communication. It is a man speaking to men, but he is not necessarily speaking about himself; he is creating something that speaks independently and for itself, something that may speak to him in its own voice as it speaks to others. The author is no more to be confused with his poem than the actor with the part he portrays on the stage. Yet no one accuses the actor of insincerity, or the character he portrays of deliberate sham, because one is so manifestly different from the other. No one in his senses would expect a painter to produce nothing but self-portraits. The ideas and feelings of a poem are not primarily personal views at all, they are part of its subject. They create a point of view to be considered for its own sake

F

and not as a communication of what the poet thinks about things, though it may also be this. Even when it is, it is meant to be a public poem in the sense in which a hymn we sing in church is a public poem. The writer of the hymn may be genuinely expressing his own religious feelings and convictions but he does not write the hymn to convey his private views. He writes in the name of all Christians what each can share as articles of a public and common faith. It would not be too much to say that the mark of a great poet is his ability to write in this public sense. The measure of his greatness is in a sense the measure of his detachment from merely personal communication, and the measure of his detachment is the measure of the sincerity of his work.

There is something in all this to be said in defence of the critics. Whether the artist aims at expressing himself or at expressing his subject, he cannot keep himself out of his work. It bears his individual stamp and cast of spirit. Crass critics tend to identify the author, the man who wrote the poem, with the person, or, to use a popular critical term of the day, the *persona* who appears in or through the poem. All poems suggest a personality which is that of the literary person the poem itself creates. A reader rightly feels that it is not the poem speaking, but *someone* who is speaking to him by means of the poem, and he forms an impression of this someone from the poem itself or from the whole body of the poet's published work. If a writer's work has coherence and consistency, from the whole body of the work a coherent personality emerges and it is to this that the critic attributes views and attitudes of mind. Sometimes, as happens with Byron, we know enough about the man in other ways to distinguish him quite clearly from this literary personality or *persona*. Sometimes, as with Wordsworth, we are able to be sure that they are nearly identical. Sometimes, as is the case with Shakespeare and with Chaucer, we can have very little idea what the man himself was like. The soldier, the courtier, the clerk of works, the customs official, the ambassador, the man responsible for the rape of Cecilia Champagne, have scarcely an echo in any of the works from the *Book of the Duchess Blanche* to *The Canterbury Tales*. The shrewd business man, the Stratford burgher, the man who left his second best bed to his neglected wife, appears so little in the personality suggested by the poems and the plays that foolish people have tried to identify the literary *persona* with so unlikely a character as Lord Bacon.

This brings me to the question of the sincerity of the poet as opposed to the sincerity of his poems. I have never really understood Yeats's doctrine of the 'poetic mask' and I doubt if anyone can, since Yeats appears to have been playing a double game with himself as well as with his readers. Not a dishonest game but a game in which the rules were largely inspired guesswork. But I think I have understood enough to be suspicious of the idea of the mask as author. Poets invent various games and legends which may be untrue but are a help in the difficult business of composition. Schiller is said to have believed that rotten apples in his desk helped the poetic process. Blake believed that his composition was a process of taking dictation from angels. For my own part, I have sometimes found it useful to pretend that the poem was writing itself and that I was merely there in the part of a midwife, though of course I knew better. To take poets too literally in their accounts of how they proceed in composition is a mistake characteristic of critics. Some writers may be helped by a clear notion of themselves as literary personalities but I think they take an undue risk.

After my first book of poems came out I decided not to read any reviews. I was perhaps influenced by the instances of friends who have had books published and have taken too much to heart what the reviews said of them. It seemed to me that they had been entangled in the images of themselves presented by the Press. No doubt a literary personality does emerge from one's own work and this literary personality or mask can become a pressure on the actual man who writes the poems. When Byron, two-thirds of the way through his writing career, decided to abandon the 'Byronism' which had made his earlier work so popular he found himself almost trapped by it. *Don Juan* upset and horrified his friends and public because it presented a new Byron, detached, witty and rather gay, and this did not fit in with the gloomy, self-regarding, wounded Titan composed of Childe Harold, Lara, and Manfred whom the public had long identified with Byron himself. In my own case I do not care to know about the literary personality that the poems create, precisely because I do not want him to impose himself on any further poems I may write. Tennyson seems to me to have been a sad case of a man largely taken over by the Tennysonian figure whom his earlier poems created—and this was to be to the disadvantage of his poetry, because the literary *persona* is not a creative person. He does not write poems. He is created by the poems, and, if the writer is too conscious of him, he can, I think, end up not writing from himself but from this factitious view of himself. In the worst cases, such as Swinburne's, for example, he may be in danger of ending by parodying himself.

More poets than we perhaps imagine perish or impair their talents in this way. Pasternak in his *Ochrannaya Gramota* mentions it as the fate of Mayakovsky and of Pushkin. Speaking of the death of Mayakovsky, he says:

I now propose to relate that strange occurrence, repeated from age to age, which might be called the closing year of a poet. Suddenly conceptions which can never know completion come to their end. . . . They change their habits, they are full of new plans, they cannot sufficiently boast of the buoyancy of the spirit. And then, all at once there is the end, sometimes violent, more often natural, though even then, in the lack of desire to fight it off, very like suicide. . . . But who will understand, who will believe that, in 1836 all at once, Pushkin saw that he was anybody's Pushkin, the Pushkin of 1836? That the time arrives when suddenly all the responses long since coming from other hearts in response to the beats of the principal heart, which also beats and thinks and wants to live, fuse together into one heart, transformed and enlarged.

A poet so trapped by the public image of himself is in great danger. He has become a society of which he is not even a director. He has abdicated that autonomous service to forces within himself which are the only source of a poet's sincerity. He has become the slave of his literary *persona*.

The Practical Critic

WE are all aware, both as readers and as teachers, of the problems involved in interpreting a poem, even an apparently simple poem. I. A. Richards a few years ago made the problem explicit when he applied experimental methods to the way readers react to poems; he showed how preconceptions and fixed demands prevent them seeing the poem as it is, and the way irrelevant associations lead to downright misreading. The results, published in his *Practical Criticism*, included a survey of the various types of inadequate readers: the reader who insists on being too literal-minded, the reader who judges every new poem by an old favourite, the reader who condemns a poem because it asks him to think as well as feel, the opposite kind of reader who despises a poem if it is too easy and does not need solving like a crossword puzzle, the reader with a cut-and-dried critical theory, and the reader who wants a poem to give him a sentimental work-out. Practical criticism has now become a commonplace of the academic study of poetry.

Unfortunately the results have not always been up to expectation. Criticism in these years has undoubtedly become sharper and more probing, more conscious of the implications of judgments passed and the nature of critical processes. But it has also suffered from a certain over-confidence, amounting, among what are known as the New Critics, to arrogance; this arrogance is due in the main to assurance in the method supplied by practical criticism, an assurance of having been given an infallible instrument capable of a scientific determination of values. The poem is always under the critic's microscope, and he seems never to reflect that while he is testing the poem the poem may in fact be testing him. Sometimes, if he were aware of it, a very sardonic eye is gazing back at him through his lens.

Because most of the poets so examined are dead, and because those who are alive are often naturally shy of explaining a poem which they expected to explain itself, I have sometimes thought that it would be amusing to do some practical criticism in reverse and that is what I intend to do here. I have taken one of my own poems and subjected the comments of three of Australia's best and best-known critics on this poem, to the processes of practical criticism. The three are old friends of mine and by no means arrogant as men or as critics. All of them hold distinguished academic posts as teachers of English, and two of them are, in addition, practising poets of great distinction.

First of all, here is the poem:

Imperial Adam

Imperial Adam, naked in the dew,
Felt his brown flanks and found the rib was gone.
Puzzled he turned and saw where, two and two
The mighty spoor of Jahweh marked the lawn.

Then he remembered through mysterious sleep
The surgeon fingers probing at the bone,
The voice so far away, so rich and deep:
'It is not good for him to live alone.'

Turning once more he found Man's counterpart
In tender parody breathing at his side.
He knew her at first sight, he knew by heart
Her allegory of sense unsatisfied.

The pawpaw drooped its golden breasts above
Less generous than the honey of her flesh;
The innocent sunlight showed the place of love;
The dew on its dark hairs winked crisp and fresh.

This plump gourd severed from his virile root,
She promised on the turf of Paradise
Delicious pulp of the forbidden fruit;
Sly as the snake she loosed her sinuous thighs,

77

And waking, smiled up at him from the grass;
Her breasts rose softly and he heard her sigh—
From all the beasts whose pleasant task it was
In Eden to increase and multiply

Adam had learned the jolly deed of kind:
He took her in his arms and there and then,
Like the clean beasts, embracing from behind,
Began in joy to found the breed of men.

Then from the spurt of seed within her broke
Her terrible and triumphant female cry,
Split upward by the sexual lightning stroke.
It was the beasts now who stood watching by:

The gravid elephant, the calving hind,
The breeding bitch, the she-ape big with young
Were the first gentle midwives of mankind;
The teeming lioness rasped her with her tongue;

The proud vicuña nuzzled her as she slept
Lax on the grass; and Adam watching too
Saw how her dumb breasts at their ripening wept,
The great pod of her belly swelled and grew,

And saw its water break, and saw, in fear,
Its quaking muscles in the act of birth,
Between her legs a pigmy face appear,
And the first murderer lay upon the earth.

It may be useful to set down what I can remember of the way this poem came to be written. As far as I remember, since it must be over ten years now, it was a poem that in one sense wrote itself. That is to say it was not written to a plan worked out beforehand as is generally the case with me. At least I have for the most part a complete idea of the poem I want to write even though I may not have much detail in mind. But this was not so with 'Imperial Adam'. In this case I had been re-reading *Paradise Lost* and writing some lectures on it; in particular I was concerned with the moral, theological and human problems concerned in the

Fall of Man and the various arguments of the critics about this central incident, particularly those of C. S. Lewis and A. J. Waldock. The great poem was still brooding over me like a cloud but I had a sense of relief at putting it behind me for a time. A few days later I was walking to work when a phrase came into my head quite casually and unexpectedly: Imperial Adam! I began thinking of Adam as the founder of the whole empire of man upon the earth and of all that history records of that empire. I thought also of the curious irony of the ruler alone without a Kingdom to rule, and yet, I thought, by his nature, with its taint of original sin which his action passed on to the whole of mankind, he possessed, ruled and directed them before they were born. The whole of history was implicit in Adam as a plant is implicit in the genes of the seed before it germinates. While I was idly thinking about this—much more vaguely, of course, than I have set it out here—the first line came into my mind:

> Imperial Adam, naked in the dew,

When I got to my office, I wrote it down, and some days later I sat down to see if something could be made of it. My only intention was to give a picture of Adam waking on a fresh sunny morning and finding naked Eve beside him. It was to be a picture poem, and that is mainly the way it came to be written. First, I thought, Adam would lie half-awake remembering what seemed to him a strange dream, then he would wake and turn over and discover his new partner, and because love is natural and they were alone in the world they would love each other and love would lead to making love, and making love would lead to conception of a child and conception to birth and the first child to be born was Cain.

> And the first murderer lay upon the earth.

There was no intention in this except to indicate the irony of the fact that Cain was, in the story and in fact, a murderer. It seemed to me amusing, and the whole poem was intended to have a tone of quiet amusement: God behaving like a surgeon removing a diseased part, the fact that the body of man and the body of woman resemble each other and differ in such a way that one could be considered a parody of the other, the fact that if woman could be considered as she was in medieval theology as the temptress of man, then Eve could be represented as combining the characters of the serpent and the forbidden fruit in herself, the fact that Adam, when he came to make love, would be inexperienced and base his practice on that of the animals— all those things struck me as pleasant, ironic and amusing ideas, and I was pleased, when I had finished the poem, with what I thought was its probable effect: a *jeu d'esprit*, a way of having a little gentle fun with the ancient story—in fact a sort of holiday relief from several weeks of hard work in which I had been engrossed in the serious issues of Milton's great epic.

Moreover I should like to repeat that the poem was never conceived or planned as a whole. While I worked on each stanza I had no idea of what was coming next. The poem came fairly easily but only after I said to myself: well, what next? As I remember, my main preoccupation was to find something that would keep up the tone of what I had already written. I rejected several ideas which seemed to me to give too serious a tone on the one hand and too facetious a tone on the other. The last line came as a surprise. The poem was never intended to lead up to it and I only thought of it at the last moment. When I did I nearly rejected it as being a bit too smart—but thinking it over I decided to keep it because its irony was, I thought, in keeping with the irony of the whole. I really believed that the irony would be obvious to any reader and that nobody would be likely to take the poem too seriously, or as anything but what it was meant to be: a picture as richly sensual as I could make it, infused with an amused and detached irony of occasional ideas.

I am not simple enough to imagine that a poet must always succeed in doing what he imagines he is doing when he writes a poem. His actual achievement is likely to fall short of his intentions, and sometimes it may exceed his intentions—if he is lucky. On the other hand I do not subscribe to a popular view in some modern criticism which holds that what a poet means to do is quite irrelevant to the interpretation of the poem. If a writer is reasonably competent then he will have enough command of his language and his ideas to know what he is doing and, unless he is singularly vain, he ought to be able to judge whether he has in fact done what he thought he was doing. But a poem once written and published must stand on its own feet. All that the reader can gather of the poet's intentions must come from the poem itself. The art of reading *is* an art. It cannot be an exact science. Even the simplest poem can be interpreted in more than one way and to some extent the interpretations are valid if they can be supported by the text. There are sometimes absurd and inadequate interpretations which are not valid at all, but there is no sharp line dividing the valid from the invalid reading. Each reader comes to a poem with a different background of reading and experience, images in the poem connect with images and experiences which he may not share with the author or with other readers; ideas in the poem react on ideas and systems of belief which may be quite other than those in the mind of the man who wrote it. So that no two readers will read quite the same poem. To some extent each re-creates it as he reads.

Nevertheless if a poem is not a mere machine for starting private fantasies, if interpretation is not to be quite arbitrary, there must be a means of keeping the process well within limits and it is the job of a competent poet to provide those limits in the coherence and structure of the poem itself. It is the job of a competent reader to stop himself at the point where the poem gives him no warrant for an interpretation, however attractive or interesting, that may occur to him. Now I have given you a little more about this poem, 'Imperial Adam', than a reader usually has to check his interpretation by. The three critics whose remarks follow did not have this additional information. Let us see what they made of it, not as critics, because I am not concerned with their judgment, but as readers. As readers they have read the same poem with care and interest and yet have come to very different conclusions, and these conclusions have influenced their critical views. The first exhibit is from the pen of James McAuley ('The Pyramid in the Waste' (*Quadrant*, Vol. v, No. 4, 1961, and *Australian Literary Criticism*, ed. Grahame Johnston), Oxford University Press, 1962).

As I read it, the ground-structure of assumptions and valuations in Hope's poetry is the Manichean inheritance, presumably mediated by Calvinism. This is the starting point, but what actually develops thereafter is quite complicated: it is an attempt to establish a new structure of assumptions and valuations different from either Manicheism or Christian orthodoxy. . . . The critical instance for my interpretation is the poem 'Imperial Adam', in which the Adam and Eve legend is re-written to give a different account of the Fall. Matter, the flesh, sensual enjoyment and sexuality, are presented in all their glowing delight. Yet they are also presented as the direct and immediate source of the appearance of evil and guilt. The wills of the two are entirely naive and innocent. But the fruit of their fleshly delight is guilt and death: not as the result of disobedience, or misuse of natural appetite, but simply by instinctive and normal use. The birth of the murderer Cain at the end of this glowing rhapsody is not just a gratuitous shock effect: it is the consummation of the poem.

Now, in advancing this poem as evidence, I am in the delicate and temerarious position of contradicting the poet's own reading. The problem is not that the poem celebrates the natural splendour of the material creation. That I can allow for, as we shall see. The difficulty is that, in a letter in reply to my advancing this interpretation (in an admittedly incomplete form), the poet amicably began, 'Probably you are right about "Imperial Adam",' but went on to say: 'But I did not mean it that way. I meant to put a case for the spontaneous generation of evil from things not in themselves evil at all—rather like the occurrence of lethal mutations in biology.' If I nevertheless do not give up my point, it is because I am concerned with the pressure—almost automatic and unconscious—of a mode of interpreting reality which can persist underneath many surface manoeuvres. The assumption that such a pattern exists is necessary if one is to make sense of Hope's poetry.

How explain the vehemence of its reactions, unless one knows what it is reacting against; how explain its metaphysical torment, which is something more than the record of personal grief and ill-starred love? Finally, in regard to 'Imperial Adam' in particular, what is the point of the following description of Eve?

> *This plump gourd severed from his virile root,*
> *She promised on the turf of Paradise*
> *Delicious pulp of the forbidden fruit;*
> *Sly as the snake she loosed her sinuous thighs . . .*

By the identification with the forbidden fruit and the serpent, Eve's body becomes the source of evil. Notice too that at this point the shadow of something not naive and innocent touches the scene in the 'slyness' of the amorous invitation.

What we must now place in its significance is the celebration of sensuality which (in alternation with images of disgust) is a feature of Hope's poetry:

> *The pawpaw drooped its golden breasts above*
> *Less generous than the honey of her flesh;*
> *The innocent sunlight showed the place of love;*
> *The dew on its dark hairs winked crisp and fresh.*

Now, in the first place, it is to be observed that the adult Hope is an unbeliever, an atheist Manichee. The whole conception of the 'spiritual' is imperilled, and the spirit has certainly no heaven to go to after liberation. . . . Half at least of the Manichean scheme has collapsed. There is earth, and a hell, which is really the psychic underworld of nightmare and dread and slavery to instinct, a dimension of this life. Where, in such a universe, is to be found the principle of grace, of transcendence, of reconciliation and reintegration? This is the point at which the poems come face to face with nihilism and despair. In a Manicheism turned atheist there would seem to be no solution.

The writer was perhaps misled by my statement that I intended the poem to put a case for the spontaneous generation of evil from things not in themselves evil at all. I should have added that I did not write the poem with this intention at all, but that, once it was written, I thought it could be interpreted in this way. This, however, hardly matters, since the interpretation he gives it is one that he

came to before I answered his query, and which he maintained in spite of it. It is an interpretation which sees the
poem as an expression of a Manichean point of view. I
don't know much about Manichean beliefs but I understand
that they regard the material world, and particularly the
human body, as essentially evil and a source of danger and
corruption to the soul. Sexual love, as the supreme celebration of the energies of the body and of the material world,
is therefore the greatest of evils and must be looked on by
the spiritual man with disgust and repulsion. According to
McAuley the poem expresses this disgust and fear of sex and
the evil of the material world, and expresses it in the ambiguous form of celebrating the delight of the sensual and
the sensory, its love and attraction, and at the same time
attacking it with savage irony. As a poet I am therefore like
a hopeless drunkard contemplating a bottle of whisky, yearning for it, dwelling on the satisfaction of drinking, and feeling fear and disgust for the inevitable attack of *delirium
tremens* that must follow; disgust at the result and fear
because he knows that he cannot resist.

McAuley may be right, though I hope he is not. One might
argue that a poet can be actuated by motives of which he is
not aware and can write poems with meanings that he never
realizes. But my point is that a good reader must find the
evidence in the poem itself. He may then support that
evidence from outside, but it seems to me that McAuley proceeds the other way about. He has convinced himself from
what he knows about me and from reading other poems of
mine that I am a Manichean and an atheist. He then finds
evidence in the poem to support these views and in the
process has ignored evidence—for example the tone of amusement, my poor jokes—which do not fit in with the view.
Finally, having convinced himself on what he actually finds
in the poem because it *is* there, though it is not the whole
of what is there, having distorted what is there in parts by
neglecting the way the parts are related to the whole, he
goes on to find things that are not there at all: an underlying denial of spiritual values, of grace, and of belief in a

principle of transcendence and reconciliation. It is a typical case of misreading a poem by coming to it with a ready-made set of beliefs to which one makes the poem conform. One of McAuley's leading tenets, as a critic, is that modern poetry, modern art and modern beliefs are infected with Manichean principles which they derive from a Protestant heresy, in particular from puritanism which tended to regard man as totally depraved and the flesh as inherently evil. This sort of criticism is always suspect because it is essentially arbitrary. A Hindu or a Marxist approaching the same poem in the same way from a different point of view could give a quite different interpretation. The Hindu could see it as a working out of *karma* and an illustration of the Great Wheel of Being. One can imagine a Marxist seizing on the title. Adam is an imperialist and imperialism is evil. Adam has lorded it over the beasts in Paradise and now he lords it over Eve. He takes possession of her as his private property, and by that act symbolically initiates bourgeois society. See how aptly the poet shows the solidarity of the proletariat against their exploiters when the pregnant animals combine to help poor Eve and see how Adam's imperialist behaviour leads to social disruption and murder.

You can in fact always find what you are looking for in almost any poem, if you read it the way you want to read it. Modern criticism has as its besetting sin a tendency to be too subtle and to interpret poems in ways that they will not bear.

Now let us look at what Vincent Buckley has to say, in his *Essays in Poetry*:

> Hope's poems are concerned with objective situations and . . . he imposes his logical order on them by making them as much like events as possible. We see the use of such a method in 'Imperial Adam', a poem which has an ironic twist in the last line, but which pays attention to other human realities besides the paradoxical way in which joy seems to beget horror. In evoking the atmosphere of the garden of Eden, Hope treats the situation of Adam and Eve not as a mere piece of symbolism, but as a set of events; and he uses his poetic form to give those events the kind of logical sequence which events must have if they are to be properly understood.

In its combination of strong formal control, rich sensuous perception, and extremely precise diction, this is remarkable among modern poetry. There is no need to defend my statement about its chief qualities. It has the air of passionate and most pointed utterance avoiding rhetoric by a sheer control of form; and that control is achieved, as I have been insisting, by treating the poem's situation as a sequence of events, and giving them the authority not only of the author's manner, but also of their own strong logic.

Buckley's interpretation is obviously different from Mc-Auley's. He, like McAuley, is a Roman Catholic but he does not bring his religious beliefs to bear on the poem. He is perhaps on sounder ground because he takes the poem to deal with an objective situation—that is to say, it is not a mere symbolizing of personal attitudes and problems, but an attempt to let events speak for themselves. It simply presents the paradox of the way joy seems to beget horror in human life and leaves it to the reader to interpret what this can mean. He does not, like McAuley, try to find an interpretation of the fact in the poem itself.

Nevertheless the use of the word 'paradox' suggests a bias in the reader's interpretation which is perhaps not justified by the poem. *Paradox* suggests contradiction—logically irreconcilable terms asserted together—the implication is that there is something contradictory in the idea that joy should beget horror, that innocent and natural love should produce a child who will bring unnatural death into the world. Good can only beget good, and evil evil. Now, if anything, the poem regards this not as contradictory or paradoxical but as perfectly natural. It is ironical that this should be so, but there is nothing contradictory about it. The fact that we act in innocence has nothing to do with the results of our actions, which may prove good or evil. Abel was a good man, though tactless; Cain was a bad man. Both were children of Eve.

This misconception in Buckley's case does not rest, as it does in McAuley's, on importing his preconceptions into the poem, the crudest cause of misreading; it depends on what I believe is a failure to observe the *tone* aright. When the critic says that the poem avoids rhetoric by sheer control of form I do not know just what he means. But he seems to imply that it only just escapes being rhetorical or that one does feel a rhetorical manner in it though it is controlled enough not to be offensive. If by rhetoric he means declamation, then one can see why he takes the last line to be proposing a startling paradox instead of ironically presenting a simple and obvious fact. This can only be the result of failing to observe that the situation is presented with some degree of humour and detachment, and this is stressed by the critic's insistence that the tone of the poem is one of passionate utterance. Once again he may be right, but I could only reply that, if so, I have failed to communicate. It is a common fault of poets, of course, to misjudge their achievements, but I feel quite remote from the poem now, and re-reading it my impression is that there is enough evidence in the language to allow an intelligent reader to detect the element of amusement which makes it unlikely that the tone is one of passionate conviction or concern.

Now I take my third exhibit, from S. L. Goldberg's 'The Poet as Hero' (*Meanjin*, 1957):

> There is probably a certain amount of calculation in Hope's treatment of sex, a desire to *épater le bourgeois*; . . . and yet, when these things have been said, there do remain grounds for unease. . . . That different attitudes appear in different poems is neither here nor there; what is more to the point is that these attitudes are not always reconciled in the poetry. Perhaps two poems best illustrate this. The first is . . . 'Chorale', . . . the second is 'Imperial Adam' where the flow seems deeper to the extent that it is a larger and richer poem. Its symbol is the first intercourse of Adam and Eve in Eden, and it is filled with what is comparatively rare in Hope, a *warmly* sensuous awareness of physical life. Its tone is quiet, grave, reverential; its theme the ambiguity of sexual passion—at once free and joyful, yet even in paradise 'forbidden fruit'; creative, yet giving birth to destruction. We may wonder what is implied by 'forbidden

fruit' in Eden, and why one event that would seem very relevant, the Fall, is only vaguely referred to, but it is the melodramatic touch of over-insistence in the last line that most clearly betrays the poem's failure to resolve the double aspect of its theme.

S. L. Goldberg is a literary critic but not, like the other two, a practising poet. His is a mind of great subtlety and analytic power. His is also a thoroughly academic mind in the best sense. He will not accept a work of literature, whatever its reputation and however speciously pleasing it may be, until he has tested it thoroughly for what he regards as the essential qualities of cohesion, sense, coherence and wholeness. He has noticed the implicit comic intention and he allows the poem to speak for itself unimpeded by preconceptions or ready-made theories. He sees that its intention is neither to be declamatory, didactic, nor passionate, but a warm and sensuous enjoyment of a picture presented for its own sake. But, unlike Buckley, he is not willing to accept the surface impression of a poem made up of a series of events each of which leads logically from the one before it. He demands, quite reasonably, that a poem should have a theme, and that the theme should be as coherent as the exposition. The theme, he says, is 'the ambiguity of sexual passion—at once full and joyful, yet even in paradise "forbidden fruit"; creative, yet giving birth to destruction'. This ambiguity, he holds, must be resolved in the poem if the theme of the poem is to be consistently and coherently presented, and the melodramatic last line, the over-insistence on the destructive outcome of sexual passion, shows that it is *not* resolved.

One might reply that the poem gives no real warrant for the view that sexual passion is ambiguous and leads to destruction. It is what it is, and destruction is what it is. One is not causally connected with the other at all except in a purely mechanical sense. One can eat a good dinner and have a stomach-ache afterwards. The stomach-ache may be caused by the dinner, and it is unpleasant. But it would be false to argue that the pleasure of eating is an ambiguous pleasure containing a hidden element of indigestion. It is what it is, and one may have the same pleasure at another time without suffering for it afterwards.

But this is not very much to the point. The point is that, even if one accepts Goldberg's view, he is making demands on the poem as a structure which there is no reason for him to make. Why should every poem which presents us with a problem be required to offer a solution of the problem? Why should a poem be a failure if it presents an ambiguous situation but not a resolution of the ambiguity? Its purpose may well be to pose a question rather than to find an answer. It may even intend to present us with the fact that sexual love *is* ambiguous, and that it is in the nature of things that there is no resolution of this ambiguity, or that the double nature of love is a cause for joy rather than despair. The intellectual joy of apprehending the mystery of things as they are may in fact be the very 'resolution' at which the poem aims. As I said, I make no such claims for this poem. It had no such theme in mind. Its aim, if any, was just to be a poem: to present a situation with as much sensuous impact as possible, and to protect the reader from taking it as a poem with a 'message', by a certain irony and humorous detachment. This is true of many poems even when they may appear to have an underlying theme or even an overt message. It is not always wise to take these at their face value. The poet may be misconstrued if he is taken to be using his poem as a means of communicating an idea, because the idea may have no more than dramatic value. It may be a part of the structure and not a hint to show us what the structure is meant to convey. The dancer Pavlova, it is said, was once asked what was the meaning of a certain dance. 'If I could have put it into words,' she said, 'I would not have needed to dance it.' Dancing and music, especially music, are arts in which we are used to the idea that the *meaning* of the music or the dance in each case is simply what it *is* and nothing more. In the criticism of poetry, however, we are not so used to the idea that the meaning may be no more than what the poem *is*. It is perhaps chiefly the defect of academic criticism that it is unwilling to accept this. It would not dream of asking: what is the meaning of a rose; what deeper themes are its structure and beauty intended to convey to us? Because many poems are symbolic and do intend us to take a message from them, the academic critic is often apt to ignore any poem which is just like a rose, a structure beautiful and satisfying in itself and content for this to be its only meaning.

I have taken three examples of what seem to me failures in reading. I may, as I said, be wrong. I make no claim to infallible insight. The point is not to prove my critics wrong but to suggest that the only safe attitude and the most fruitful and rewarding approach to poetry is to be at once tough-minded and humble, to question a poem closely but to realize that a poem also has questions to put to us and that those questions may be more searching than our own. We cannot help coming to it with preconceived beliefs and demands. That is only human nature. We cannot help putting interpretations on it that may not be justified, and poems are often ambiguous. If we take the view that we are there to interpret the poem we are likely, with the best will in the world, to misread it. But if we take the view that the poem is there also to challenge our preconceptions and our critical theories, that in a certain sense it is there to help us interpret or reinterpret ourselves, then we shall be more likely to be good readers and good critics—we are more likely in that famous phrase of Yeats to have added to ourselves what was not in us before. 'When I have read a poem', said Yeats, 'I have not added to my knowledge: I have added to my being!'

I hope my three friends will not think it unfair of me to use their comments in this way or that my readers will not think it unbecoming in a poet to answer his critics so, or to seem to act as sponsor to his own work. I do indeed hold that poets should be silent and that poems should speak for themselves if they can. But in an age of criticism it is sometimes fitting not to let the critics have it all their own way.

Poetry, Prayer, and Trade

FEW people nowadays concern themselves with the old question of the proper subjects for poetry. Probably they do not think it worth discussing since there seems to be general agreement that no subjects are improper for poetry, that no field of human experience is outside the poet's range if he cares to venture on it and that above all there are no specifically 'poetical' subjects. For all that, poets seem remarkably timid about breaking into new fields. A few years ago it was the mark of a modern and up-to-date poet to write about factories, slums and other aspects of the industrial wastelands, but this was no more than a return from the vegetable and rural interests popularized by the romantic poets, an exploration of another side of the life of society which has, as a whole, always been open to poetry. And even so, nobody seems to have found the world of commerce and business enterprise attractive except a few poets of the left who felt themselves in duty bound to sneer at it in the interests of the class struggle. That determined vein of minor poetry which in the eighteenth century tried to extend the range of Virgil's *Georgics* by writing edifying poems on the art of preserving health, the wool-trade and the raising of sugar cane, petered out. Erasmus Darwin's attempts to bring the new territory of descriptive science within the range of poetry found no followers. *The Botanic Garden* was not a success, but then Darwin was not much of a poet and a frontal attack on the science of botany was in any case an ill-advised venture. There are other ways of setting about it but the poets have shown little interest in exploiting them. The divorce between literature and science which began in the seventeenth century had no more than the force of a *decree nisi* until the end of the eighteenth. By the end of the nineteenth century it was practically a *decree absolute*. The poets of today are not expert in the sciences and few scientists are, like Mr Alex Comfort, also poets. C. P. Snow is probably crass in talking of the Two Cultures of our society. He might have called them the two half-cultures and been on safer ground.

The treasures of knowledge, the vast new resources for the poetic imagination which lie in the discoveries of science, remain practically untouched by creative writers. Science has transformed the picture of the world which is their subject, and most of them ignore its offerings. They are confined within the field of *belles-lettres*, and what they know of the sciences is what any reader of science fiction knows. Of course there is just too much to know. The great divorce took place, in part, because it became increasingly impossible after the seventeenth century for any man to take all learning as his province. Poetry, which Sir Philip Sidney could claim, with some justice, to be the queen of the sciences, has had to abdicate her throne and retire into private life. She has lost her former standing in every part of the world of learning. Nobody today really expects a poet to know anything about anything. People read poetry to be entertained, to cultivate their sensibilities, to elevate or sharpen their feelings, to extend, reassure or confirm their emotions. No one goes to poetry to be informed, to be taught the great general truths which Dr Johnson considered it the essential function of poetry to illuminate with 'the wide effulgence of a summer noon', or to take a synoptic view of the nature of things. This was Peacock's complaint in *The Four Ages of Poetry* and it was a just complaint. Shelley's magnificent reply was more a statement of what poetry ought to have been doing, than of what it was actually doing. And few of the poets of today have any claim to knowledge or wisdom beyond that of the ordinary citizen. If they speak on philosophy or natural science, they speak as amateurs and without authority. Because they have no authority, they can hardly claim to be 'legislators of mankind' whether acknowledged or not. To do them justice they make no such claim, but in consequence they have for the most part withdrawn from the field of public concerns and confined themselves largely to topics of private interest and personal sentiment. The question of what, among the whole range of human affairs, may be considered proper subjects for poetry, and of whether the range of poetry has limits or not, is therefore of no interest to them, for they have already imposed and accepted their own limitations, as the index to any current anthology will suggest.

Yet the question of the proper field of poetry has not always seemed unimportant and it is still worth considering. Dr Johnson was of the opinion that poetry had both an upper and a lower limit to its range of subjects and that these limits were prescribed by the nature of poetry, from which we might deduce what it was capable of doing and what it was not. In his 'Life of Milton' he argues that the soul's communion with God in prayer is above the proper reach of poetry.

> Contemplative piety, or the intercourse between God and the human soul, cannot be poetical. Man, admitted to implore the mercy of his Creator, and plead the merits of his Redeemer, is already in a higher state than poetry can confer.

Johnson, I suppose, would not deny that a prayer cannot be put into the form of a poem; his point is that the artifice of composition, the attention required by the form, are inconsistent with that entire submission of the mind and the heart to their sole object which the act of prayer essentially demands. For the essence of prayer is not supplication, confession, acknowledgment of grace, praise or contrition, but undivided *attention*, a conscious opening of the heart to what it is about to receive, a holding of the will towards union with a higher will. Its object is something that no act of the will can make specific, no proposition of the mind or the imagination can set before themselves. The attitude of prayer is a stillness, a standing with the head bowed, the body kneeling or prostrate. But poetry is David dancing before the sacred ark.

It is therefore not to the point to answer Johnson, as he has been answered, that the act of prayer and the act of composition need not necessarily take place at the same time any more than we would expect all love-poems to be written in bed. Nor would it be entirely cogent to argue that if poetry is, as it should be, a language natural to a poet, he may as properly pray in his language, as other men may pray in theirs. Johnson's objections have a real force, not limited by his main contention that prayer is too sacred an activity to be within the reach of a profane skill. Poetry is a secular occupation even when its subject is religious, and, in fact, it may deal with any matter of faith so long as it does not actually pretend to pray. The communion of man with God belongs to another realm in which art is irrelevant and disruptive.

At the other end of the scale he holds that poetry also has a natural limit. His remarks on the insuccess of *The Fleece* in his 'Life of Dyer' show that in his opinion trade and commerce come below this limit.

> When Dyer whose mind was not unpoetical has done his utmost, by interesting his reader in our native commodity, by interspersing rural imagery and incidental digressions, by clothing small images in great words, and by all the writer's art of delusion, the meanness naturally adhering and the irreverence habitually annexed to trade and manufacture, sink him under insuperable oppression.

Once again Johnson's position may seem vulnerable. *The Fleece* has its moments and although Johnson's views are on the whole just, Dyer's mistake might seem to have consisted simply in trying to apply 'all the writer's art of delusion' to his subject. Had he treated the wool-trade simply, truthfully and without trying to inflate his subject he might have treated men in their ordinary occupations with more sense of their significance for the life of man as a whole, more insight into the mystery of the life of nations, of which the science of economics gives an integral though a superficial interpretation.

But Johnson again is right in his judgment, even if his reasons appear questionable. For Dyer is trying to do something which it does not belong to the province of poetry to do—his latter-day *Georgics* attempt, by adding to trade the charms of poetry, to promote the wool industry of Great Britain and incidentally by encouraging the use of wool to discourage the importation of silk from France. It is not because Dyer uses his art to promote something—some of the greatest poems do the same—nor that he uses it to promote British commerce, that he goes beyond the limits poetry should observe. It is rather that the poetry does not grow out of the subject but is added to it, as Johnson observes, to give commercial interests a specious charm. It falls, innocently enough, into the class of those advertising ploys which give away plastic aeroplanes with packets of breakfast food, or recommend the virtues of a shiny new motor-car by showing it with an equally shiny blonde in a bathing suit beside it.

It is in this way that we can perhaps determine the limits of subjects for poetry, for there seem to be some, and commerce is one of them, which are arid and infertile material. Poetry cannot be made to grow out of the subject except by a *tour de force* which we may admire more for its ingenuity than the conviction it produces. Poets instinctively avoid such subjects except as material for satire. Satire can operate on them successfully because its theme does not grow from the material itself but from a perception of the inadequacy, the inherent barrenness of the matter and the false values that have grown up around it. Sport is perhaps another such subject. As practised in the modern world it is imbued with such inherent vulgarity that Johnson's criterion may apply. Yet one would hesitate to assert that a poet of genius could not cultivate something worth while even from the most unpromising material. If the material of the sciences has so far proved intractable, it is not so much that it is inherently barren ground, as that poets have used the wrong approach. They have tried, as Darwin did, to apply the resources of poetry to the raw material instead of making the poetry grow naturally out of the interest and significance of the material, thereby transmuting it into the proper stuff of poetry.

Poetry does not deal with its subjects in the abstract. Its central subject is man in all his aspects, social, moral, psychological, biological and individual. Outside this it deals with the universe in its relation to man. But its specific and distinguishing character is that whatever aspect of its subject it treats, its central concern is to present it under the aspect of eternity, to present us with the metaphysical image of creation, to bring out the poetic meaning of things. It would be absurd, of course, to demand of every poet and every poem that it deliberately explore the metaphysical possibilities of its subject or philosophize its subject in any crass way. Its mode of operation is more likely to be implicit than explicit. A true poet is more likely to be unconsciously than consciously metaphysical in his vision of the world. He is so by the bent of his nature as a poet, and only secondarily by deliberate intention. But a man who has continually before him a vision of the world as a whole, whose mind naturally dwells on and seeks to grasp the complexity, the variety and the mystery of the world of man as a whole, who has as his interest a sense of the past, the present, and the future as one process, a man continually obsessed with the passion for a synoptic view, cannot write the slightest of poems on the most particular of themes without reflecting this ruling passion in his treatment, perhaps quite unconsciously, and perhaps the better for its being unconscious. It is this which gives poems, not in themselves either metaphysical or even reflective, their effect of presenting things *sub specie aeternitatis*. Eternity may never be mentioned. It is a light, itself unseen, by which one sees the quality of the object in a way that the temporal light of practical interests can never show it. The poet making use of the matter of biology is in no sense competing with a text-book of biology. He is eliciting its proper music.

The idea of a philosophical poem is a case in point. The great philosophical poem has haunted the European tradition since the beginning and it has largely remained a ghost in spite of the natural affinity between the philosophic and the poetic cast of mind. The versifying of a philosophic system has rarely been successful in spite of the example of Lucretius. Poets have tried all sorts of devices. They have embedded it in the matter of epic as Milton did, in auto-biography as Wordsworth did, in a theological travelogue as Dante did. They have fleshed it with allegory like Phineas Fletcher or with an invented mythology like Blake and Rilke. All these examples are instructive of the methods by which poetry can use the material of an intellectual system. But perhaps the most instructive is a frontal attack, the *Nosce Teipsum* of Sir John Davies. The comments of some critics show that they think of *Nosce Teipsum* as a *tour de force*. Davies they feel has succeeded remarkably well in making his intractable material seem poetic; but that is all. C. S. Lewis, for example, says:

> . . . his *Nosce Teipsum* is, like Greville's Treaties, an un-adorned and genuinely didactic poem. In this versified essay on the nature of the soul there is no question of using science as a peg on which to hang poetry. It is a perfectly serious text-book in which the arguments are as lucid as prose could make them. The writer's talent appears in the success with which, while keeping our noses to the grindstone, he yet gives us a sort of pleasure by the verse . . . the work as a whole produces admiration rather than pleasure.

Some of these remarks are very just. To be able to argue lucidly in verse, especially on a highly technical subject, and to make the verse at the same time produce the effect of poetic statement and of harmonious and delightful move-ment, is a great achievement. Dryden is our great master of argument in verse that is as lucid as prose and is effective as poetry, but Davies is not far behind him in this rare skill. He lacks Dryden's energy and vigour; he sacrifices force to a smoothness that tends to become cloying, but the task he set himself was more difficult than any that Dryden ever attempted. Davies really does write in the form of a theologi-cal treatise. His method is quite scholastic, setting out first the nature and functions of the soul in separate sections, proposing his argument, raising the possible objections and

variant theories and arguing them out to a definite conclusion before raising the next heading of his subject. The
second part, in which he argues for the immortality of the
soul, is equally scholastic and methodical. It is naturally not
as rigorous or as detailed as the arguments of St Thomas
Aquinas on the same topics in nearly two thousand pages of
the *Summa Theologiae* or in the one hundred and twenty
pages or so of the later treatment in the *Summa Contra
Gentiles*, but the method is essentially similar. It is all based
in a similar way on scripture, Christian theology, and Aristotle's treatise on the soul, the *De Anima*.

But when all this has been said, the more important aspect
of the poem has not been mentioned and this is where C. S.
Lewis seems to be quite astray. It is a successful treatise in
verse. But it is much more than a treatise. It is a genuine
poem and as a poem its mode is one of celebration rather
than of argument and exposition, though it is that as well.
It celebrates the prime fact of human nature as the age
understood it, the fact that man and man alone among
earthly creatures was a rational and immortal being. 'For on
the earth no other wights there are that have these heavenly
powers but only one.' It is this sense of triumphant celebration which is everywhere implicit in the verse and makes it
very much more than a versified essay. There may indeed be
no question of using science as a peg on which to hang
poetry, as Lewis says, but this does not mean that the science,
which is certainly there, is devoid of poetry or, as he suggests,
that the pleasure the verse contrives to give is a kind of
clever trick by which he makes a dry scientific argument
more or less palatable. A look at the text almost anywhere
in the poem shows that the poetry is an integral part of the
argument and it may be worth while to see just how this
comes about.

What Lewis has missed is the fact that this lucid argument,
which has many of the virtues of good expository prose, uses
in fact devices which are not those of prose at all. There is
a good deal of plain statement in diction which only differs
from that of prose in that it moves to a sustained poetic

rhythm. But the proper ornament and imagery of poetry is consistently used throughout. The whole poem is alive with imagery, but the most remarkable thing about it is that the imagery always serves the abstract line of argument and is subordinate to it in such a way that the feeling of plain exposition is never threatened. We may take, as an example, one of the most rigidly technical passages in the poem; that in which Davies describes the relation of the senses to the faculty of imagination.

Aristotle in his *De Anima* explains at considerable length in abstract scientific language how the various senses bring, through bodily organs, their impressions to the soul. The faculty of imagination then combines these sensations into an *image*, the image of the object in the outer world. The active intellect next compares and contrasts individual objects and abstracts from these their universal forms or essential natures, and the contemplative intellect is then able to perceive and understand the universal relations and general laws of cause and effect, and so arrive at an understanding of the structure and nature of the material world. Davies uses the word *Wit* for the intellect, both active and contemplative, and the word *Fantasy* for the image-forming faculty, the imagination. See now how he expresses this idea in poetry:

> *The Wit, the pupil of the soul's clear eye*
> *And in man's world the only shining star,*
> *Looks in the mirror of the Fantasy*
> *Where all the gatherings of the senses are.*
>
> *From thence this power the shapes of things abstracts*
> *And them within her passive part receives*
> *Which are enlightened by that part which acts*
> *And so the forms of single things perceives.*
>
> *But after by discoursing to and fro*
> *Anticipating, and comparing things*
> *She doth all universal natures know*
> *And all effects into their causes brings.*

First we may notice the way the arid argument is transformed by the images of the clear eye with its pupil. The intellect is to the soul as the eye is to the body, the source of light and comprehension, but it is more than this, for it not only receives; it sheds light by making clear the essential nature and primary laws of the world which the senses and the body only receive as a crude picture of individual objects. The intellect illuminates the world of sense and, further, the image of the star suggests the celestial nature and origin of the soul. This profound but quite unobtrusive poetic image is followed by the image of the imagination as a mirror, the philosophic, *Speculum Naturae*. It is this device of apt and intelligent imagery and the tactful but appropriate personification that runs through it all; by this device the poet transforms the dry argument of his original into an intellectual drama to which the sustained harmony of the verse gives the character of a celebratory hymn. It is done by almost precisely the same means employed by St Thomas Aquinas to make pure poetry out of the abstract dogmatic theology with which he packs every line of his great hymns for Corpus Christi Day, 'Pange, Lingua Gloriosi' and 'Verbum Supernum Prodiens'. I say, almost exactly, for there is a rich compression and a majestic force in St Thomas's language to which Sir John Davies cannot pretend: *Nosce Teipsum* suffers perhaps, because of its length, from the unvarying smoothness of its verse, and a certain rational tameness of language. It is, for all that, a most remarkable poem. It illustrates the essential mode of poetry and the essence of the means by which subjects usually thought of as intractable and refractory may be assimilated to that mode.

Frost at Midday

WHAT was it that ruined Coleridge as a poet? He was undoubtedly a poet, and he was undoubtedly ruined and knew it. Some talk of opium, some of ill health, and some of instability of character. Coleridge himself was apt to attribute it to metaphysics. All these may have had a part in the ruin of his powers and his inspiration, but for myself I am inclined to think that the chief cause was Wordsworth, and in particular Wordsworth's views of the inspiring and restorative force of natural scenery and rustic life.

When the two men met, each was unhappy and each was isolated in his unhappiness, and their friendship, which was immediate and intense to the point of rapture at first, was based both on a sympathy of ideas and temperament and on the relief of having someone to talk to who seemed really to understand. Each moreover could contribute something to the other. What Wordsworth principally needed was encouragement and recognition, someone with a disciplined mind and a philosophic training who could discuss and criticize his ideas, and someone to give him confidence and assurance by providing an intelligent echo for ideas which otherwise would die on empty air. But Wordsworth was an impervious, strong, and dense character, energetic, organized and purposeful. Nothing really influenced or changed him. Coleridge on the other hand was easily captured and captivated, unsteady in purpose and looking for someone to worship, and Wordsworth was perfectly ready not only to be worshipped but to draw up a creed and a ritual for his worshippers. In his letters and throughout *The Prelude* he professes a deep affection for Coleridge, but Coleridge in *his* letters professes a sort of boyish hero-worship of Wordsworth. His view just after meeting Wordsworth remained much the same until their estrangement: 'Wordsworth is a very great man, the only man to whom *at all times* and in *all modes of excellence* I feel myself inferior.'

In 1813, after the quarrel, he writes in another letter of his 'fifteen years of such religious, almost superstitious idolatry' of Wordsworth. Wordsworth's feelings for Coleridge were always well on this side of idolatry, in fact after five or six years even the adoring Coleridge was known to remark that he detected 'crying instances of self-involution' in Wordsworth. Coleridge's adulation and self-abasement were excessive. He had no need to feel in every way inferior to Wordsworth, and his usual powerful good sense deserts him in this. As he later came to realize, he was a much greater and more perceptive critic than Wordsworth. He had all round a better mind, a higher order of intelligence and, at their best, his gifts of imagination and of poetry were certainly not inferior to Wordsworth's. Yet it was only after he met Wordsworth that these gifts came into full bloom. Before this Coleridge had written quite a lot of poetry, respectable enough in its way, but respectably dull, moralizing or enthusiastic in a rather embarrassing way—besides a good deal of arch, humorous or sentimental verse. Without the excitement and imaginative impetus that his early association with Wordsworth gave him, I think it possible that we would not have had 'Christabel' or 'The Ancient Mariner' and possibly we would not have had 'Kubla Khan'. Wordsworth seems to have been able to keep Coleridge going, to put a rein on him and prevent him from flying off at tangents so that he was not always being diverted by new projects and never managing to finish any. Even as it is, 'The Ancient Mariner' is the only first-rate poem that Coleridge managed to finish. 'Christabel' was abandoned, and 'Kubla Khan' is only a fragment of the original two to three hundred lines which Coleridge remembered on waking from his dream.

But if Wordsworth inspired Coleridge, he also, I feel, diverted him from his true bent. Wordsworth seems to have converted Coleridge to his religion of Nature and to his theory of Nature as the true and original source of poetic inspiration. Coleridge had written a fair amount of descriptive nature poetry before he met Wordsworth but it was in the mild and gentle descriptive strain of William Lisle

Bowles, whose sonnets Coleridge tells us he so much admired. A good example is 'Lines on an Autumnal Evening' written two years before he met Wordsworth. It is a fairly conventional use of a natural setting as an ornamental background to a meditation on love. But in 1800 we find Coleridge, in a letter, lecturing William Godwin, who is coming to visit the Lake country and its poets, on the moral and spiritual value of mountain scenery. It is 'nutritive'—mountains nourish the soul:

> They put on their immortal interest then first, when we have resided among them, and learnt to understand their language, their written character and intelligible sounds, and all their eloquence, so various, so unwearied. . . . Here, too, you will meet Wordsworth 'the latch of whose Shoe I am unworthy to unloose.'

The reference to Wordsworth gives us Coleridge's state of mind, and the remarks about mountains sound very like a pupil repeating the master's lesson.

I think that scenery, although Coleridge derived a mild pleasure from looking at it, really meant very little to him. When Hazlitt tells us of walking with him he gives a splendid description of Coleridge engaged in endless talk—the talk is mostly about books and authors—but Coleridge appears to have paid little attention to the scenery except when his attention was drawn to it. There are several passages in Coleridge's letters in which he records how little, as a child or as a grown man, the evidence of his senses meant to him, how completely his imagination had always been absorbed by books, and fired by them. In a letter to Thomas Poole written in 1797 he tells of his childhood:

> I remember that at eight years old I walked with him [his father] one Winter evening from a farmer's house, a mile from Ottery, and he told me the names of the stars and how Jupiter was a thousand times larger than our world. . . . I heard him with a profound delight and admiration: but without the least mixture of wonder or incredulity. For from my early reading of Faery Tales and Genii etc. etc.—my mind had been habitu-

H

ated *to the Vast*—and I never regarded my *senses* in any way as the criteria of my belief. I regulated all my creeds by my conceptions not by my *sight*—even at that age. Should children be permitted to read Romances, and Relations of Giants and Magicians and Genii?—I know all that has been said against it; but I have formed my faith in the affirmative.—I know no other way of giving the mind a love of 'the Great' and 'the Whole'.—Those who have been led to the same truths step by step, thro' the constant testimony of their senses, seem to me to want a sense which I possess.

The puzzle about Coleridge is that his best poems are so unlike the others. They might almost have been written by a different man; and the imagery and ideas of 'The Ancient Mariner', 'Kubla Khan' and 'Christabel' have nothing to do with realistic description or close observation of man and nature, they are all wild and imaginative, the creating of a landscape and persons within the mind itself. We have a fairly full list of the books Coleridge read and even, from his notebooks, of passages that struck him particularly. John Livingstone Lowes has been able to show in detail how 'Kubla Khan' and 'The Ancient Mariner' were composed, how subconsciously all sorts of details and imaginative suggestions from Coleridge's reading fused and animated one another in his mind, and finally issued in these magnificent dream creations. They owe nothing to the Wordsworthian practice of looking at nature and keeping one's eye steadily on the object—so well exemplified by the two lines Wordsworth contributed to 'The Ancient Mariner':

> *And he is long and lean and brown*
> *As is the ribbed sea-sand.*

This was not the way Coleridge's mind worked at its best. Much more typical of his genius is:

> *And all should cry, Beware! Beware!*
> *His flashing eyes, his floating hair!*
> *Weave a circle round him thrice*
> *And close your eyes with holy dread,*

For he on honey-dew hath fed,
And drunk the milk of Paradise.

This passage owes nothing to observations conducted in the English countryside.

Wordsworth had one of the two essential gifts of the poet in a very high degree: the sensory imagination. What he touched with his senses fired him and combined in forms of beauty and vision. He was often defective in the other essential gift of the poet, the verbal imagination. With Coleridge it was almost the other way about. Ideas, books, things put into words were the true source of his inspiration, and I believe that, like Blake, he could have said: 'Natural objects always did and now do weaken, deaden and obliterate imagination in Me.' This is very pertinent, for Blake's comment was on Wordsworth's poem, 'Influence of Natural Objects in calling forth and strengthening the Imagination.'

There is a letter from Coleridge to his wife in which he says:

> As I seem to exist, as it were, almost wholly within myself, in *thoughts* rather than things, in a particular warmth felt all over me, but chiefly felt about my heart and breast; and am connected with *things without* me by the pleasurable sense of their immediate Beauty or Loveliness, and not at all by my Knowledge of their average value in the minds of people in general . . . so you on the contrary exist almost wholly in the world *without* you, the Eye and the Ear are your great organs, and you depend on the eyes and *ears* of others for a great part of your pleasures. . . .

These passages, which speak clearly enough, are supported by the evidence of Coleridge's poetry. Wordsworth, I think, succeeded in persuading Coleridge, against his better knowledge of himself, to try to be an eye-and-ear man like himself. Coleridge's letters during the years of their association, full of notations of natural objects in the best Wordsworthian manner, show at least that the pupil knew what to look for and what to feel enthusiastic about. But the notebooks for the corresponding period tell rather a different story and, apart from a few poems such as 'This Lime-tree Bower My Prison' and 'Frost at Midnight', Coleridge never succeeded in the descriptive school.

Wordsworth himself was aware that his pupil was far from apt. About 1819 Coleridge recalled his criticism of the 'Hymn Before Sunrise in the Vale of Chamouni'. Wordsworth had described one passage as a specimen of the Mock Sublime, and Coleridge while defending his poem admits

> Yet on the other hand I could readily believe that the mood and Habit of mind out of which the Hymn rose—that differs from Milton's and from Thomson's and the Psalms, the source of all three, in the author's addressing himself to *individual* Objects actually present to his Senses, while his great Predecessors apostrophize *classes* of Things, presented by the Memory and generalised by the understanding—I can readily believe, I say, that in this there may be too much of what our learned Med'ciners call the *Idiosyncratic* for true Poetry. For from my very childhood I have been accustomed to *abstract* and as it were unrealise whatever of more than common interest my eyes dwelt on; and then by a sort of transfusion and transmission of my consciousness to identify myself with the Object.

Certainly the Hymn is not a successful attempt at the sort of realization of the object required by the master's theory and practice, and Coleridge is unconsciously amusing as he describes the result, for him, of looking steadily at the object: the object disappears.

> *O dread and silent Mount! I gazed upon thee,*
> *Till thou, still present to the bodily sense*
> *Didst vanish from my thought: entranced in prayer*
> *I worshipped the Invisible alone.*

Writing to an unknown correspondent sixteen or seventeen years later, he speaks of the different course he would take 'if ever I should feel once again the genial warmth and stir of the poetic impulse'. But by then it was too late. Coleridge had ruined himself in more ways than one, and he knew well enough that the genial warmth and stir would not return. In 1825 in another letter he described the decay of his creative faculties and ascribed it partly to the deadening effect of Nature. Nature and Mind are spoken of as rivals, but what Coleridge is comparing is in fact what I have called respectively the sensory and the verbal imagination:

> It is a flat'ring thought that the more we have seen, the less we have to say. In youth and early manhood the mind and nature, are as it were, two rival artists both potent magicians and engaged like the King's daughter and the rebel genii in the Arabian Nights' Entertainments, in sharp conflict of conjuration each having for its object to turn the other into canvas to paint on, clay to mould, or cabinet to contain. For a while the mind seems to have the better in the contest, and makes of Nature what it likes, takes her lichens and weather-stains for types and printers' ink, and prints maps and facsimiles of Arabic and Sanscrit MSS on her rocks . . . transforms her summer gales into harps and harpers, lovers' sighs and sighing lovers, and her winter blasts into Pindaric Odes, Christabels and Ancient Mariners . . . but alas! alas! that Nature is a wary wily long-breathed old witch, tough-lived as a turtle and divisible as the polyp, repullulative in a thousand snips and cuttings, *integra et in toto*. She is sure to get the better of Lady *Mind* in the long run and to take her revenge too; transforms our today into a canvas dead-coloured to receive the dull featureless portrait of yesterday: not alone turns the mimic mind, the ci-devant sculptress with all her kaleidoscopic freaks and symmetries into clay, but *leaves* it such *clay* to cast dumps or bullets in.

By this time Coleridge could diagnose his own case, but it was, as I say, too late. But it might not have been too late in 1805 when Coleridge wrote the passage which called forth such disapproving comments from Walter Pater in his essay on Coleridge:

> In looking at objects of nature while I am thinking, as at yonder moon, dim-glimmering through the window-pane, I seem rather to be seeking, as it were asking, a symbolical

language for something within me, that already and for ever exists, than observing something new. Even when the latter is the case, yet still I have always an obscure feeling, as if that new phenomenon were the dim awaking of a forgotten or hidden truth of my inner nature. While I was preparing the pen to write this remark, I lost the train of thought which had led me to it.

Pater, as Humphry House has pointed out, did not quote the passage either accurately or honestly. He omitted a good deal between the last sentence and what precedes it here, and so makes it appear to refer to something other than what Coleridge intended. But the original is not so different that Pater's comment is not pertinent. He seems in fact to be furious with Coleridge for not looking, like a true Wordsworthian, steadily at the object. 'What a distemper of the eye of the mind,' he exclaims, 'what an almost bodily distemper there is in that!' And he is right, but for the wrong reason. It is not the disease of Coleridge's imagination that prevents his being inspired by the moon, but the moon which distempers his imagination. At this moment Coleridge is getting healthy. He is almost at the point of pulling down the blind, shutting out the damned moon, and taking up one of those books of travel which had the power to set his creative mind to work. Instead, one fears that like a conscientious pupil of Wordsworth he forced himself to write a painstaking and feeble poem, 'Ode on the Impression of Moonlight Shining over My Neighbour's Pigstye!'

The remarks prefaced to 'Kubla Khan' show better how Coleridge found his inspiration and under what circumstances it best found release:

In the summer of the year 1797, the Author, then in ill health, had retired to a lonely farm-house between Porlock and Linton, on the Exmoor confines of Somerset and Devonshire. In consequence of a slight indisposition, an anodyne had been prescribed, from the effects of which he fell asleep in his chair at the moment that he was reading the following sentence, or words of the same substance, in *Purchas's Pilgrim-*

age: 'Here the Khan Kubla commanded a palace to be built, and a stately garden thereunto. And thus ten miles of fertile ground were inclosed with a wall.' The Author continued for about three hours in a profound sleep, at least of the external senses, during which time he has the most vivid confidence, that he could not have composed less than from two to three hundred lines; if that indeed can be called composition in which all the images rose up before him as *things*, with a parallel production of the correspondent expressions, without any sensation or consciousness of effort. On awaking he appeared to himself to have a distinct recollection of the whole, and taking his pen, ink, and paper, instantly and eagerly wrote down the lines that are here preserved.

What seems important here is the phrase 'at least of the external senses'. Coleridge's poetic imagination for once operated independently. Whether he was actually asleep or not, his external senses were suspended in their operation and the verbal imagination took over from the passage he had been reading in Purchas as the laudanum began to take effect:

In Xamdu did Cublai Can build a stately Palace, encompassing sixteene miles of plaine ground with a wall, wherein are fertile Meddowes, pleasant Springs, delightfull Streames, and all sorts of beasts of chase and game, and in the middest thereof a sumptuous house of pleasure, which may be removed from place to place.

From there, as Professor Lowes has shown in *The Road to Xanadu*, his dreaming mind, by a marvellous chemistry of association, gathered from other memories of his reading all the elements which the poem combines and transmutes. The enchanted youth and the damsel with the dulcimer come from another book by Purchas in which he describes the Paradise of Aloadine, the Old Man of the Mountain, prince of the Assassins. Mount Abora, the sunny pleasure dome with caves of ice, Alph the sacred river, the woman wailing for her demon lover, come from a dozen other places, and were all combined and reintegrated through that imaginative fusion which Coleridge called 'esemplastic power'. It is no mere scissors and paste job. It is an entirely new and brilliant creation that the dreamer's mind brings together from these bits and fragments. As Lowes says:

> They are at once the same and not the same, as you and I have known their like to be a hundred times in dreams. Nobody in his waking senses could have fabricated those amazing eighteen lines. For if anything ever bore the infallible marks of authenticity it is that dissolving panorama in which fugitive hints of Aloadine's Paradise succeed each other with the vivid incoherence and the illusion of natural and expected sequence and the sense of identity that yet is not identity, which are the distinctive attributes of dreams.

Nothing that Coleridge ever wrote conveys such a sense of vivid and magical pictures in the mind—such an impression of intense and brilliant vision. Yet note that not one detail comes from the direct observation of nature which Wordsworth's theory demands. Every least detail has been traced to its source, and every one came, not from Coleridge's observation, but from his reading. It is a warning against dogmatic theories about poetry. For precisely the opposite was usually true about Wordsworth's best poetry.

Coleridge rarely achieved these moments of integration of all his powers. Even without the disturbing influence of Wordsworth he was only a poet by fits and starts. He found himself in one of these sterile patches after finishing his translation of Schiller's *Wallenstein*. He turned with relief to continue 'Christabel' but 'Christabel' would not come.

> . . . the deep unutterable Disgust which I had suffered in the translation . . . seemed to have stricken me with barrenness for I tried and tried and nothing would come of it. I desisted with a deeper dejection than I am willing to remember. The wind from Skiddaw and Borrodale was often as loud as wind need be—and many a walk in the clouds on the mountains did I take; but all would not do—till one day I dined out at the house of a neighboring clergyman, and some how or other

drank so much wine, that I found some effort and dexterity requisite to balance myself on the hither Edge of Sobriety. The next day, my verse making faculties returned to me and I proceeded successfully. . . .

All one can say is that it is a pity Coleridge did not take fewer Wordsworthian walks and that he did not get drunk more often, whether on his neighbour's wine or his neighbour's books. 'Kubla Khan' was released by opium, the first part of 'Christabel' by a vision, the second by his neighbour's wine and 'The Ancient Mariner' by the thing that intoxicated Coleridge more than anything—good talk about books with a sympathetic and appreciative friend.

To me, the saddest document in this unhappy story is 'Dejection: An Ode', written in 1802, when Coleridge's powers were still intact, though at a point when he clearly realized that they were in danger. In this ode, with unusual insight, he describes the nature of the danger, and almost succeeds in admitting that Wordsworth is his evil genius.

At the time the poem was written, Coleridge was very unhappy. He had been in miserable health for some months, he was unhappy in his married life, and even more unhappily in love with Sara Hutchinson, and for some time he had been oppressed by a feeling that poetry had left him. For this he blamed all these misfortunes, but particularly metaphysics and his wife's ill temper.

The ode plainly went through several revisions before it reached the form in which it is printed in Coleridge's collected works. The first of which we have knowledge is a verse-letter to Sara Hutchinson dated 'April 4, 1802, Sunday Evening'. This was during a visit from Wordsworth, who had just begun the composition of his 'Ode on Intimations of Immortality'. Wordsworth, following his usual habits, probably read these first four stanzas to Coleridge, whose own ode seems to have echoes of its language and its theme. A few weeks later Coleridge wrote to a fairly recent friend, William Sotheby, quoting long sections of the verse-epistle as a poem addressed to Wordsworth. When the poem appeared, in the *Morning Post* later in the year, it was transformed and given its present title. The person then addressed was 'Edmund' who is plainly Wordsworth. In the final version, published fifteen years later, the person addressed is an anonymous 'lady'. The first version has two main topics: first, Coleridge's domestic unhappiness, his hopeless love for Sara and his concern about her health, and, second, the loss of his creative powers as a poet. In the printed version most of the private and domestic matters have been dropped, and the poem is confined to the theme of the poetic imagination, its source and its decay. His critics have on the whole assumed that this was due to Coleridge's sense of fitness and that his addressing the published poem to an anonymous or pseudonymous recipient was due to the same feeling. Most of them seem to feel that the poem was originally addressed to Sara Hutchinson, and that she is the 'lady' addressed in the final version. I think there is reason to doubt these assumptions. In the letter to Sotheby, Coleridge is quite explicit. He says the poem was written in an actual state of dejection, and that it was written to Wordsworth, and goes on at once to quote a passage which seems to echo the opening of Wordsworth's ode:

> There was a time when meadow, grove and stream
>   The earth and every common sight
>   To me did seem
>   Apparelled in celestial light,
>   The glory and the freshness of a dream.
>   It is not now as it hath been of yore;—
>   Turn whereso'er I may
>   By night or day,
>   The things which I have seen I now can see no more.

Coleridge may be taken to reply:

>   Yes, dearest Poet, yes!
>   There was a time when tho my path was rough
>   No day within me dallied with Distress
>   And all Misfortunes were but as the Stuff
>   Whence Fancy made me Dreams of Happiness:
>   For Hope grew round me, like the climbing Vine,

And Fruit and Foliage, not my own seem'd mine.
But now Afflictions bow me down to Earth—
Nor car'd I, that they rob me of my Mirth;
But O, each Visitation
Suspends what Nature gave me at my Birth,
My shaping Spirit of Imagination!

There is no reason to disbelieve Coleridge's statement that the poem was written to Wordsworth. Wordsworth and Dorothy had been with him for nearly a week when he wrote to Sara, and he is likely to have heard the first few stanzas of the Immortality Ode on the first day they were there, for William was never slow in giving his friends the benefit of a reading from his latest compositions. The version Coleridge sent to Sotheby has a number of differences from the letter to Sara. These suggest that he either was quoting from memory or was transcribing from another version. There is no possible reason to think he was lying to Sotheby, and the simplest solution to the problem is to suppose that the poem was indeed written in the first instance to Wordsworth, being called forth by Coleridge's dejection and despair and the spirit of joy which is stressed in Wordsworth's ode. On the fourth of April, when, as Dorothy remarks in her journal, they all 'sate pleasantly enough after supper', Coleridge, we must suppose, retired and wrote his long verse-letter to his beloved Sara and incorporated the poem or part of the poem he had already written to Wordsworth; or perhaps he changed and added to the poem to Wordsworth so as to make it a letter to Sara. In its different forms it was in fact addressed to both. When he made the poem public he omitted those parts which were of a strictly private nature in each case, but the poem in its public form is addressed to Wordsworth under the name of Edmund.

If the poem is taken as addressed in the first instance both in its private and its published form to Wordsworth and not to Sara, and if we suppose that it was evoked as an answer to the opening section of the Immortality Ode, then it seems to support the view I have been taking. It is in fact a most complex poem in which there are at least three voices speaking, sometimes at once, sometimes in turn. There is Coleridge talking to 'dearest William' describing the scene and his state of mind; there is Coleridge talking to himself and trying to probe the secret cause of his distress and his failure; there is the almost unconscious cry of the fettered and baffled spirit within, uttering the real reason, which Coleridge himself fails to acknowledge.

If we take the version that, later in 1802, first appeared in print, and change the pseudonymous Edmund for the direct references to Wordsworth in the letter to Sotheby, what Coleridge tells his friend is that he has lost the power to respond to the beauties of Nature.

> I see them all so excellently fair,
> I see, not feel, how beautiful they are!

He goes on to reject at least half of Wordsworth's theory of poetic inspiration. Nature does not inspire. Nature has no life of her own that supports ours and is the source of poetry. The glory and the freshness of the dream we have in youth is not something we receive from Nature and grow blind to later. It is something we bring to Nature and lose if we do not foster it ourselves.

> O Wordsworth! we receive but what we give,
> And in our life alone does Nature live:
> Ours is her wedding garment, ours her shroud!
> And would we aught behold of higher worth
> Than the inanimate cold world allowed
> To the poor loveless, ever-anxious crowd,
>   Ah! from the soul itself must issue forth
> A light, a glory, a fair luminous cloud
>   Enveloping the Earth—

The pupil is almost in full revolt, but not quite. In the next stanza the spiritual and creative joy is traced to the source that Wordsworth traced it to: Nature is the source even if the joy is not in itself an autonomous return to Nature:

> *Joy, William! is the spirit and the power*
> *Which wedding Nature to us gives in dower*
> *A new Earth and new Heaven,*
> *Undreamt of by the sensual and the proud.*
> *We in ourselves rejoice*
> *And thence flows all that charms or ear or sight.*

Coleridge then turns to ask himself why it is that this creative joy, so largely measured to Wordsworth, has deserted him. He answers that it is caused by defects in himself: first, afflictions rob him of natural happiness and suspend his shaping spirit of imagination, and, second, in order to escape or bear his suffering he is thrown back on metaphysical speculation which destroys the creative imagination altogether.

At this point the storm, which was threatening when the poem began and has burst over the house, interrupts him. This seventh stanza appears to break the train of thought, to be a description of the storm, and to lead to the final stanza in which the poet invokes blessing, joy and peace on his friend. But the storm is not truly an interruption, it is a continuance of the theme. Early in the poem the poet had prayed for it to come:

> *Those sounds which oft have raised me, whilst they awed,*
> *And sent my soul abroad,*
> *Might now perhaps their wonted impulse give,*
> *Might startle this dull pain, and make it move and live.*

It is in fact while gazing at outward forms of Nature in this mood that he realizes their powerlessness to wake 'the passion and the life whose fountains are within'. As the poet gazes in dull misery at the peculiar tint of yellow green in the sky, the Aeolian harp beside him in the window moans and complains in the draught. When the storm reaches its height the harp responds with a scream of agony. Coleridge on another occasion compared himself as a poet to an Aeolian harp, and I believe he does so here. The wind is now addressed not only as a 'Mad Lutanist' but as a 'Mighty poet' telling a series of tragic and horrible tales, and one such as

Wordsworth himself might have told. It may be fanciful, but in this stanza I hear the underground voice accusing Wordsworth, the wind, and Nature itself, of having tortured Coleridge, the harp, and the lost child of the final tale, of being the cause of his ruin, and of denying his soul the 'sweet and potent voice of its own birth', thus reducing him to the passive condition of a harp for the mad wind to play on.

Unfortunately at this point Coleridge stops thinking. Having uttered his scream of torment and protest, he returns to the conviction that Wordsworth is right, or at least that Wordsworth deserves to be right, and he invokes blessings on his pure and deadly friend.

It was Coleridge's last chance. 'Dejection: An Ode' is his last great poem. In another two years it was all over with him as a poet. He was only thirty. 'Frost at Midday' is his epitaph.

The Argument of Arms

TOWARDS the end of Marlowe's *Tamburlaine* there is a brutal scene in which the conqueror returns from his victory over the Turkish kings and calls for his son Calyphas. As Calyphas has refused to take part in the battle his father prepares to kill him with his own hands in front of his other sons, his generals and the captive kings. Although Techelles, Usumcasane and Theridamas, the generals who have followed Tamburlaine's fortunes from the start, must surely by now be inured to massacre, arbitrary judgment and brutal execution, they are shocked. They know well enough the ungovernable temper and the ferocious resolution of their master. Yet they fall on their knees and plead for the young man's life. Tamburlaine berates them like raw recruits:

> *Stand up, ye base, unworthy soldiers!*
> *Know ye not yet the argument of arms?*

As they plainly do not know it, he proceeds to tell them, and concludes the lesson by stabbing Calyphas to death.

The Argument of Arms is the argument of the play, and it is doubtful whether some editors and critics of the play have understood it any better than did Tamburlaine's generals, though in both cases it is not for want of telling. It is, indeed, just of that speech in which the argument is first and most clearly set out, in poetry so splendid as to compel understanding, that understanding has been most lacking. This is, of course, the speech in the first part of the play where Cosroe, for whom Tamburlaine has won, and from whom he has then taken, the Persian throne, reproaches his conqueror, calling him 'bloody and insatiate Tamburlaine'. Tamburlaine replies:

> *The thirst of reign and sweetness of a crown*
> *That caused the eldest son of heavenly Ops,*

117

To thrust his doting father from his chair,
And place himself in the imperial heaven,
Mov'd me to manage arms against thy state.
What better precedent than mighty Jove?
Nature, that fram'd us of four elements
Warring within our breasts for regiment,
Doth teach us all to have aspiring minds:
Our souls, whose faculties can comprehend
The wondrous architecture of the world,
And measure every wandering planet's course,
Still climbing after knowledge infinite,
And always moving as the restless spheres,
Wills us to wear ourselves and never rest,
Until we reach the ripest fruit of all,
That perfect bliss and sole felicity,
The sweet fruition of an earthly crown.

Scholars and critics have often pointed out that the first part of this passage is the very poetry of Renaissance humanism, but they usually show disappointment at the end of it. John Addington Symonds called it 'Scythean bathos'; Una Ellis-Fermor, after calling the passage on the Soul perhaps the noblest lines Marlowe ever wrote, goes on:

And then, at the end, comes the inevitable bathos. To what is all this aspiration and hunger directed? 'To the ripest fruit of all' Marlowe tries to persuade us:

'*The sweet fruition of an earthly crown*'

We do not believe him. We go back to the lines about the 'faculties' of the soul and take care never again to link them with what follows. For the fact is that Marlowe has suddenly —it may be all unconsciously—broken faith with his idea. The instinct is there, magically defined and passionate. The error, the inability to grasp in a weaker mood its full significance, occurs when Marlowe attempts to give it a specific direction.

Muriel Bradbrook is equally definite:

Knowledge is infinite; that is given in the straight soaring of the 'mighty line', but the movement is not cumulative and flags to 'the sweet fuition of an earthly crown'. In fact the

whole passage about the soul and knowledge occurs as a mere
parenthesis in Tamburlaine's argument to justify attacking
Cosroe: it is flanked with prudential matter.

Frederick Boas, more perceptive, sees that the passion for
sovereignty has the same ultimate source as the insatiable
scientific impulse and the quest for beauty. But he fails to
see that not only have these passions the same source, they
are in fact said to be the same passion. The argument is one
argument, and only if it is taken as one argument has the
play meaning and coherence. Marlowe is under no mis-
apprehension, has no doubt that to be a king is a higher
felicity and a greater aspiration than anything else, even the
pursuit of knowledge infinite.

The notion that knowledge is the highest of human aspirations is perhaps peculiarly a scholar's delusion and, in an
age which worships knowledge, it is natural for scholars to
misunderstand the passage in question. And this is especially
so since kings have now fallen into such disrepute that to
aspire to sovereignty over others has come to be regarded as
a disgraceful if not actually a criminal ambition. But Marlowe's contemporaries would have had no trouble in understanding Tamburlaine's drift, though they might not have
understood the view of man and the world that underlies his
argument. The humanism of this passage is in fact far removed from the humanism of the study or the laboratory. It
is the humanism of war, a view in which all human values
are determined by war alone.

What Tamburlaine says to Cosroe in effect is this: 'You
think my conduct that of a barbarian and a greedy thief. On
the contrary my action in making war upon my king and
taking his crown was that of a god and made with the motive
and the understanding of a god. For the gods may be assumed
to know the nature of the world and they know that its
principle is that of war. War is only incidentally destructive
and disruptive. In essence it is the principle of order, the
principle of beauty, and the principle of knowledge. The
gods who established the world and their rule of it, did so
by war. The whole state of Nature is one of perpetual strife.

1

The elements of which our bodies are composed are in a state of constant strife and the order and growth of those bodies is the product of the strife. The same is true of the soul and its faculties, of the frame and structure of the world which the soul by its nature desires to comprehend, and of the social order in which each man has his place. That place is determined by strife and the highest human achievement is to become the master of men, the only being whose will is entirely free, the only being whose values are absolute in fact as well as in aspiration.'

The metaphysical conception on which the play is based is this theory of a universe in which order is the creation of strife and values are determined by strife. It is not a modern theory of 'might is right'; it is not a Nietzschean view of the will to power. It is based on the Aristotelian view that every creature strives towards the perfection of its nature. Man is the highest of the creatures and the perfection of his nature is to rule his world. Given the law of strife, the highest state of that perfection is to rule man himself. But those who actually rule usually do so, not by virtue of their absolute right to do so, for that right has not been tested by contest. This is where Tamburlaine differs from the hereditary kings. He has the natural genius for power and he actually tests it out against all possible contenders. He achieves the perfection of human nature in a world in which only one man can be perfect. This standard of values means that the man who imposes his will on all others is, in a sense, the only fully human being among them. For he alone has achieved the full possibilities of the human. He subsumes all values into himself. It means in fact that the man who can achieve this and maintain his position must have gifts and qualities above the human. He partakes of the divine, a claim that Tamburlaine makes more than once. Usumcasane remarks:

> *To be a King, is half to be a god.*

To be supreme King of Kings certainly requires it; and in this the sole meaning and the whole beauty of life consist. Knowledge has its part but it is only a subordinate part in

this aesthetic notion of power, which links knowledge and
beauty with political supremacy.

The key to Tamburlaine's speech to Cosroe is the mention
of the war of the four elements. This is not the usual Eliza-
bethan view which, in general, stresses the harmony and
combination of the elements, under the rule of Nature;
Nature, again, is under the rule of God. But Marlowe appears to have belonged to that group of daring minds which
gathered round Sir Walter Ralegh, though he may not have
been a member of the circle when he wrote *Tamburlaine*.
Of this group Miss Bradbrook says that they

> . . . sought a 'Philosophic Theology' and for this purpose
> they turned to the classics for help in the synthesis. They were
> driven to those early writers whose sayings were most conveni-
> ently to be adapted to their own situation. They began with
> Stoicism . . . the stoicism of Plutarch and Seneca. But the
> Stoics had included a good deal of the doctrine of such esoteric
> writers as Heraclitus of Ephesus and his sayings can be divined
> behind the poetry of Marlowe, Chapman and Raleigh.

Marlowe's was a thoroughly original and independent
mind, but if we do need to find a source for an unusual idea,
it is very possible that he might have been struck by the
remark in Plutarch's *Moralia*:

> Heraclitus . . . says that Homer in praying on the one hand
> that strife might perish from among gods and men, was [on
> the other] unaware that he was praying against the occurrence
> of all things since from battle and antipathy they have their
> beginning.

He might also have come across a passage in Aristotle's
Eudemian Ethics in which Heraclitus is made to comment
on the same speech of Achilles with the statement that without opposites there would be no attunement or harmony in
the universe, that is to say that order depends on strife. And
in the same work of Plutarch he could have come on the
statement, even more pertinent to the theme of *Tamburlaine*: 'Heraclitus named war, without reservation, father

and king and lord of all things.' Marlowe's knowledge of Greek has been questioned, and there is little evidence that he read the Church Fathers, but, had these views of Heraclitus been in question, there were plenty of contemporaries who could have referred him to Origen's quotation from Celsus:

> Celsus says that the men of old used to hint at a sort of divine warfare and that Heraclitus said as follows: We must know that war is common (to all) and justice is strife and that all things happen by strife and necessity.

But whether Marlowe thought of it for himself or caught a hint from Heraclitus, it is on some such theory that the Argument of Arms is based, and it is only if we see it based on this sort of theory that the play is whole and coherent and not a series of barbarities and absurdities relieved, but hardly redeemed, by great poetry.

I imagine that the reason why the view of life on which *Tamburlaine* is based has been overlooked is simply the fact that it is so strange and so repugnant to most minds that it would never occur to them to take it seriously. The mere notion of accepting, even for the sake of argument, a thorough-going morality of power, aesthetics of power and logic of power, with its implication that only one man can achieve the end of life and that society is entirely subordinated to producing and promoting that man, these are ideas which the mind boggles at entertaining. And when it does so, many of the events in the play are bound to appear senseless, extravagant or merely revolting.

Dr Boas, for example, boggles at the massacre of the virgins of Damascus. It is, he says:

> . . . a glaringly unsuitable prelude to the immediately following lyric invocation of 'fair Zenocrate, divine Zenocrate' mounting line by line to the superb rhapsody, in which the romantic impulse ever-yearning after an unrealizable perfection finds its expression once and forever.

This might be true if we were justified in taking the 'romantic impulse' as the source of the speech. But this is what Tamburlaine disclaims. What he is talking about is the *power* of beauty arising from its actual perfection, not from any unrealized ideal. It is this power which alone can conquer the conqueror of the world, and this disturbs him. It has, he says, 'troubled his senses with conceit of foil' more than any of his foes in the field of battle. He is driven to ask how beauty fits into the Argument of Arms:

> *What is beauty, saith my sufferings, then?*

And his reply is as follows:

> *If all the pens that ever poets held*
> *Had fed the feeling of their masters' thoughts,*
> *And every sweetness that inspired their hearts*
> *Their minds and muses on admired themes;*
> *If all the heavenly quintessence they still*
> *From their immortal flowers of poesy,*
> *Wherein as in a mirror we perceive*
> *The highest reaches of a human wit—*
> *If these had made one poem's period,*
> *And all combined in beauty's worthiness,*
> *Yet should there hover in their restless heads*
> *One thought, one grace, one wonder, at the least,*
> *Which into words no virtue can digest.*
> *But how unseemly is it for my sex,*
> *My discipline of arms and chivalry,*
> *My nature, and the terror of my name,*
> *To harbour thoughts effeminate and faint!*
> *Save only that in beauty's just applause,*
> *With whose instinct the soul of man is touched,*
> *And every warrior that is rapt in love*
> *Of fame, of valour, and of victory,*
> *Must needs have beauty beat on his conceits,*
> *I thus conceiving, and subduing both,*
> *That which hath stopt the tempest of the gods,*
> *Even from the fiery spangled veil of heaven,*
> *To feel the lovely warmth of shepherds' flames,*

And march in cottages of strowed weeds,
Shall give the world to note, for all my birth,
That virtue solely is the sum of glory,
And fashions men to true nobility.

The parallel between this speech on beauty and the previous speech on kingship is clear enough. In both, the precedent of the gods is invoked. In the one the war of nature within and without produces the harmony of the body and the soul and the universe which the mind cannot rest till it knows, and this same restless search for knowledge is what leads the soul to the highest felicity of all, the supremacy of power. Science and sovereignty are each part of the same process, but sovereignty is the crown of knowledge. In the other speech, it is the same thing that prompts the ever-restless poets and all men to aspire towards the beauty they celebrate. Poetry represents the highest achievement of human genius, but perfect beauty is something beyond that genius, as sovereignty is beyond knowledge. The end of the speech is ambiguous. Some scholars think the text corrupt. But it is plain enough that after we have placed sovereignty and beauty as the two supreme human aspirations, beauty has a power to subdue sovereignty, and this, Tamburlaine argues, would be shameful except that beauty only subdues sovereignty as a means to inspire and complete it. It is the completion of the man of power by the concept and possession of beauty in which the perfection of his nature, his *virtue*, consists. It is for this reason that Tamburlaine, who won Zenocrate at the beginning of his career, defers his union with her perfection until he has achieved his own. The Argument of Beauty completes and gives sense to the Argument of Arms.

There is of course nothing romantic in this, no yearning after an unrealizable perfection in the principal actor. Tamburlaine leaves that to the poets as he leaves the yearning after infinite knowledge to the scientists and the sages. In spite of the evocation of the beauty of Zenocrate in the exquisite speech that follows immediately on the slaughter of the Damascus virgins, there is no softness, no *gemütlich-keit*, in this conception. Tamburlaine is moved by Zeno-crate's tears, but the moving itself testifies to the power of her beauty which the pleas of the youthfulness, innocence and beauty of the virgins have not possessed. It is appropriate for Tamburlaine to praise Zenocrate while the girls dangle on the spears of his soldiers before the eyes of their parents. The virgins perish in their lesser degrees of beauty and appeal as the other kings of the earth perish in their lesser degrees of force of character and genius for arms. In fact it is wrong to talk of degrees in this world, for it is a world in which what is not perfect is without meaning and without value. There is no middle way and no compromise in such a world. Beauty is the rival of beauty as force of force, and only the supreme and perfect survives. Defeat, like victory, is total, absolute, final.

Some such view makes the play in its two parts a single and coherent whole, which on other views it is hard to main-tain. The first part of *Tamburlaine* may appear coherent and complete even to those who do not see its theme. The hero sets himself a goal and that goal is achieved when he proves himself capable of defeating the greatest monarchs, and marries Zenocrate. It could be taken as a simple success story. It is the continuation in Part II which has often been criticized as a mere accumulation of battles, conquests, mur-ders and disasters, ending arbitrarily when Tamburlaine dies. As his death has nothing to do with his conquests, and his conquests in this part of the play seem to have little to do with one another, Marlowe has been accused of filling out Part II with an unrelated series of sensational incidents for the edification of an uncritical audience. Actually it is con-trived to carry the Argument of Arms to its conclusion.

The first part of *Tamburlaine* may be called the triumph of life—the triumph of life conceived as the fruition of human nature in the one man capable of achieving the per-fection of the human in terms of power. The second part might be described as the triumph of death. It opens many years after the conclusion of Part I. Tamburlaine's sons are almost grown up. He has extended his conquests to a point where even his generals are now great emperors in their own right, carrying out their own careers of conquest; and all belongs to their master. But there are still combinations of enemies against him; there are still vast regions of the world unconquered and Tamburlaine knows that he cannot rest till he has conquered them. His neighbours know it too, and so war begets war as one combination of kings after another tries to crush him. The effect of the battles, sieges and campaigns of Part II is not meant to form, like those of Part I, a connected plot. They form instead a series like the waves of a slowly mounting sea, so that we feel that Tamburlaine's presence in the world and his purpose is to bring the world to a final crisis, a great Armageddon of the nations. In these wars, in this apparently senseless and wholesale slaughter, we are made to feel ever more and more strongly the picture of human history as seen from the point of view to the Argument of Arms. Individual human life ceases to have any meaning and the nations themselves rise, fight and are destroyed like individual men. The sole meaning of the process seems to be that it produces its Tamburlaine; for the significance of man, the significance of history is its Tamburlaines.

The fact that these wars have nothing to do with the death of Tamburlaine is precisely their point. Had he died in battle he would have lost his significance. He would simply have been one of the innumerable waves in their meaningless succession. Orcanes conquers Sigismund today. Tamburlaine conquers Orcanes tomorrow; Callapine revenges his father by conquering Tamburlaine the day after; and nothing has any permanent meaning or importance. The point about Tamburlaine is that he is and remains unconquerable. He is justified in claiming a superiority that is almost divine. But he is a mortal man for all that, and his servant death will turn on his master in the end. From the death of his joy, when Zenocrate dies, to the death of Tamburlaine himself we feel Fate waiting to strike. The prayers of his generals for his life are significant in their suggestion that if he perishes then all is meaningless, for he has taken all meaning into himself. If there is no morality, no beauty, no value but in absolute and supreme power, then the tragedy of Tamburlaine is the tragedy of man himself. It is here that we may wonder where Marlowe himself stands. Does he accept the argument or not? Tamburlaine the scourge of God must die, and Tamburlaine realizes that in spite of his defiance of the gods he can control neither them nor death. He realizes that he cannot live to complete his supremacy even in this world, and that his son Amyras is incapable of continuing and perfecting his work. His reference to Phaeton and to his disastrous attempt to guide the horses of the sun, shows it only too well. Even in his own terms, if Tamburlaine represents the perfection of the human, the result is failure and is bound to be failure. But Marlowe makes no comment. We are free to accept the Argument of Arms and regard this failure as the tragedy of man, or to reject it and take Tamburlaine's failure as evidence that it is unsound, the fatal flaw that makes the play the tragedy of Tamburlaine alone.

In one sense the coherence of the play resides in its poetry. Taken in terms of the action alone the play is not free of absurdity. If Tamburlaine were merely a supreme military genius, the argument which asserts his total superiority and perfection would be unconvincing. But Tamburlaine is a poet. He conceives poetry as concentrating in its highest conceivable form, the whole of beauty, imagination and music into 'one poem's period', just as he concentrates all power in himself. It is in this alliance of the poetic imagination with temporal power, in a sense their identity, that the magnanimity of Tamburlaine consists. Poetry is his medium, as power is his nature and his genius. Poetry shares the supremacy of nature, for it is the natural language of beauty, of intellect and of power, the three perfect things. It is poetry alone which makes all three comprehensible:

> *Wherein as in a mirror we perceive*
> *The highest reaches of a human wit—*

The poetry of *Tamburlaine* is indeed the poetry of power,

and the absolute morality of power which the play exemplifies is allied to the absolute standards of poetry, which it recognizes. For poetry accepts only success, and grants lasting life only to absolute success. It recognizes no gradations and no second best. What Hazlitt, in a very curious passage for an avowed republican, says of Coriolanus, is even more apt of the poetry of *Tamburlaine*:

> The language of poetry naturally falls in with the language of power. The imagination is an exaggerating and exclusive faculty: it takes from one thing to add to another: it accumulates circumstances together to give the greatest possible effect to a favourite object. The understanding is a dividing and measuring faculty: it judges of things not according to their immediate impression on the mind, but according to their relations to one another. The one is a monopolizing faculty, which seeks the greatest quantity of present excitement by inequality and disproportion; the other is a distributive faculty, which seeks the greatest quantity of ultimate good, by justice and proportion. The one is an aristocratical, the other a republican faculty. The principle of poetry is a very anti-levelling principle. It aims at effect, it exists by contrast. It admits of no medium. It is everything by excess. It rises above the ordinary standard of sufferings and crimes. It presents a dazzling appearance. It shows its head turretted, crowned, and crested. Its front is gilt and bloodstained. Before it 'it carries noise, and behind it leaves tears.' It has its altars and its victims, sacrifices, human sacrifices. . . . It puts the individual for the species, the one above the infinite many, might before right.

Those who wish to understand *Tamburlaine* should read and re-read this passage for it represents the Argument of Arms translated into the Argument of Poetry. And those who wish to understand the real nature of poetry would do well to have *Tamburlaine* by heart, for the heart of the matter is that the Argument of Arms and the Argument of Poetry are in their essence the same.

Anne Killigrew, or the Art of Modulating

THERE is a skill in poetry which has an analogy with the technique of modulation in music. A long poem of any kind cannot be sustained indefinitely at the highest level and a poet's problem is to learn to maintain the tone of the poem as a whole, while modulating skilfully from one level to another. Now that long poems are rarely attempted it is not only an art which is in danger of being lost, but one which readers and critics often fail to recognize and appreciate. Perhaps the most astonishing feat of modulation in the whole of English poetry is Dryden's ode: 'To the Pious Memory of the Accomplished Young Lady Mrs. Anne Killigrew, Excellent in the Two Sister Arts of Poesie and Painting'.

She was born in 1660, the daughter of the Reverend Henry Killigrew, chaplain of the Duke of York, an irascible clergyman who wrote some poetry himself, in Latin. She grew up to be virtuous, accomplished, handsome and charming, and became one of the Maids of Honour to Mary of Modena, the Duchess of York. She wrote poetry and she drew and painted and in both gained some reputation within the circle of the court, though she records with some indignation a malicious rumour that she was not really the author of her poems, which began to appear when she was twenty. She complains that the Matchless Orinda (Katherine Philips) had been accepted as a poet even though she too was a woman;

> *Th' Envious Age, only to Me alone*
> *Will not allow, what I do write, my Own,*
> *But let them rage, and 'gainst a Maide Conspire,*
> *So Deathless Numbers from my Tuneful Lyre*
> *Do ever flow; so Phebus I by thee*
> *Divinely inspired and possest may be;*
> *I willingly accept* Cassandras *Fate,*
> *To speak the Truth, although believed too late.*

It is obvious throughout her poems that she had quite a good opinion of herself as a poet and it is equally obvious that there was little reason for anyone to think that she had not written them entirely herself. She threw off epigrams, she wrote complimentary addresses to ladies of the court and to young gentlemen whom she admired, and to more mature gentlemen who admired her. She wrote pastoral dialogues, moral essays in verse, poems on her own paintings, pindaric odes, lyrics about love, and even began an heroic poem on Alexander the Great but dropped it, realizing that her powers were unequal to the task. The specimen of her verse that I have quoted is quite typical. She had some competence, a little wit, small experience and less originality but her verses have a modest charm, and some personal feeling comes through the conventional language and ideas. There is nothing in the poems that a nice girl with a taste for poetry could not have managed to write. When she was twenty-five or twenty-six she caught smallpox, like the Matchless Orinda with whom she chose to compare herself, and died of it. The following year her family collected her poems and published them with an engraving of a self-portrait, a Latin epitaph, and an ode in her memory by John Dryden. Dryden is said never to have met her, but he was a friend of the family. At any rate he could not have been the poet accused by gossip of writing her verses for her.

> My Laurels thus an Others Brow adorn'd,
> My Numbers they Admired, but Me they scorn'd:
> An others Brow, that had so rich a store
> Of Sacred Wreaths, that circled it before;
> Where mine quite lost, (like a small stream that ran
> Into a Vast and Boundless Ocean)
> Was swallowed up, with what it joyn'd and drown'd
> And that Abiss yet no Accession found.

There were, of course, plenty of other poets at court. Yet it could have been pleasant to think of Dryden's Boundless Ocean paying its debt to her little brook in the great ode.

For a great ode it is. Johnson said of it, and justly at the time, 'His poem *on the death* of Mrs Killigrew is undoubt-edly the noblest ode that our language ever has produced.' For manner indeed it has perhaps never been surpassed. The problem that it raises is not with the manner but the matter. Anne was undoubtedly a poet, but Dryden has surely overpraised her. If we take the matter of the poem seriously it seems to be little more than a piece of complimentary nonsense. George Crabbe, in his preface to *Tales of the Hall*, remarked:

> If there be any combination of circumstances which may be supposed to affect the mind of a reader, and in some degree to influence his judgement, the junction of youth, beauty and merit in a female writer may be allowed to do this; and yet one of the most forbidding of titles is 'Poems by a very Young Lady'.

Anne Killigrew's volume is a little better than this, but it is still very small beer. It is difficult to believe that what the 'noblest ode' proposes as its theme can consist of fulsome praise of such a very minor accomplishment.

One way out of the difficulty is to ignore Dryden's ostensible subject altogether and to say that while he pretends to be writing about Anne Killigrew he is really writing about the art of poetry. That is what E. M. W. Tillyard does in his *Five Poems 1470-1870*.

> Dryden does indeed tell us things about Anne Killigrew, that she was virtuous and gifted; that she wrote verse and painted landscapes and royal portraits; that she died of the small-pox. But the two hundred lines spent in saying this are, as information, nearly all padding, while what astonishes and delights is the wealth of imaginative invention and the glory of the verbal music.

But this will not do at all. More than half the poem consists of information which is plainly misinformation, for Dryden appears to be saying that Mistress Killigrew was really a superb poet and painter when he must have known better, and all the readers of the volume must have known that he knew it. I do not see how a poem which is half padding and absurd hyperbole can be really good, and to hold that verbal music and imaginative invention alone can make a good poem out of trivial material and false sentiments is to make poetry itself trivial. What is said and the way it is said must have a relation that the judgment can seriously accept. Johnson has perhaps indicated the secret of Dryden's method when he says:

> When he describes the Last Day, and the decisive tribunal, he intermingles this image
>
> > *When rattling bones together fly,*
> > *From the four quarters of the sky.*

It was indeed never in his power to resist the temptation of a jest.

Johnson was close enough to Dryden and still within the world of taste to which the grand manner was natural. I think he could be trusted to distinguish whether this is jest or earnest. To Johnson this sounded like a deliberate joke, and the seriousness of the ode, I think, includes and, in fact, depends on a strain of humorous irony which runs all through it. By means of this irony Dryden manages to use the form and the language of a great Baroque ode to raise a few compliments about a charming girl to the proportions of a meditation on and a celebration of the power of poetry. And, in spite of his seeming to do the exact opposite, by the underlying humorous irony he never loses the proportion due to each of two subjects—one, the reach and force of genius; the other, the girl who touched the edge of the great world of art and letters but was in no sense a genius. What he contrives to do is to make us feel that she belongs to that world in which genius rules and that this is her gift, her distinction: *that she shared in it.* What is important is that art is important; and because Anne Killigrew had her modest share in its world she is entitled to a share in its praise. Dryden's celebration of the art of poetry has a double force. What he says about poetry is exemplified and made vivid by a superb example of the thing he is celebrating. And the magnificence of the poetry is the source of a delicate irony by which he compels dissent from, or at least qualification of, what he seems to be saying about Anne as a poet. Another source of this irony is that the information he gives of her work is at variance with the praise he loads it with. Far from padding out the poem, the information is integral to its theme and essential to a modulation of its tone.

Another aspect of the poem which Tillyard neglects is the importance of its being a funeral ode. Had Dryden tried to write in this strain while Anne Killigrew was alive—deprived of the contrast of heaven and earth, he would have found his task more difficult. But, as it is, the Christian religion is his means of supporting his theme. Anne Killigrew alive was an ordinary human being, a 'nice' girl, pious and accomplished, but she is now, he believes, in heaven. Just as we can speak seriously of a quite ordinary person translated and trans- figured by the mystery of death and the assumption of eter- nity, so we can speak of a minor poetess passing into and partaking of the eternity and immortality of the whole world of art. It requires some tact to picture Mr Bones the Butcher playing a harp beside the Glassy Sea, but this is what any Christian must be able to do, and is able to do because the mortal butcher and the immortal soul are both one and distinguishable. The mortal Miss Killigrew can be pictured without incongruity putting on the immortality of that world in which her gifts and interests gave her some part. Dryden uses her Christian apotheosis with great tact to support Anne Killigrew's literary apotheosis and so manages to give a pre- cise indication of the nature of her achievement without making us too uneasy about his placing her with Homer and Virgil. 'The writer of an epitaph', as Johnson remarked, 'should not be considered as saying nothing but what is strictly true. Allowance must be made for some degree of exaggerated praise. In lapidary inscriptions a man is not upon oath.'

But the poem is not merely a funerary ode, it is also a dedicatory poem to a book of poems, a fact which at the time also allowed for a certain conventional exaggeration.

In 1692, Dryden published 'Eleonora: A Panegyrical Poem Dedicated to the Memory of the Late Countess of Abingdon', who had died at the age of thirty-three. Dryden, who had never met her, wrote the panegyric at the request of her husband. In his preface addressed to the earl he defends the extravagance of his praise and the language in which it is couched:

> We who are Priests of *Apollo* have not the Inspiration when we please; but must wait until the God comes rushing on us, and invades us with a fury which we are not able to resist: . . . Let me not seem to boast; my Lord; for I have really felt it on this Occasion and prophecy'd beyond my natural power. Let me add and hope to be believed, that the Excellency of the Subject contributed much to the Happiness of the Execution: And that the weight of thirty years was taken off me, while I was writing. I swom with the Tyde, and the water under me was buoyant. The Reader will easily observe, that I was transported, by the multitude and variety of my Similitudes, which are generally the produce of a luxuriant Fancy; and the wantoness of Wit. Had I called in my Judgment to my assistance, I had certainly retrench'd many of them. But I defend them not; let them pass for beautiful faults amongst the better sort of Critiques: for the whole Poem, though written in that which they call Heroique Verse, is of the Pindarique nature, as well in the Thought as the Expression; and, as such, requires the same grains of allowance for it. It was intended, as Your Lordship sees in the Title, not for an Elegie, but a Panegyrique. A kind of Apotheosis, indeed; if a Heathen Word may be applyed to a Christian use.

These words apply with even more force to the ode on Anne Killigrew. It is Pindaric in form as well as in nature; it is a panegyric more than an elegy; it is Anne Killigrew's Apotheosis and in it the poet is plainly transported by the multitude and variety of his similitudes which he neither intends nor expects his readers to take in too literal and sober a sense. Nevertheless the exuberance of its praise is tempered with a perfectly just insinuation of the defects of the young woman's poetry even though these defects are turned into compliments, a device Dryden had used shortly before in his exquisite elegy on the young poet John Oldham. He candidly indicates that Oldham's verse was rough and unskilled though he turns the fault to a compliment, calling it 'A Noble Error'.

To do this in the ode on Anne Killigrew without giving offence and without involving himself in contradiction, required the greatest tact and skill and the power to modulate from a tone of the most elevated fervour to one that might be described as one of familiar and ironic tenderness. He prepares for this in the first stanza which, more than any part of the poem, deserves Johnson's attribution of Horace's encomium on Pindar: *Fervet, immensaque ruit.*

This note of ironic tenderness appears immediately in the opening stanza:

> *Thou youngest Virgin-Daughter of the Skies,*
> *Made in the last Promotion of the* Blest;
> *Whose Palms, new pluckt from Paradise,*
> *In spreading* Branches *more sublimely rise,*
> *Rich with Immortal Green above the rest:*

It is, of course, very delicately insinuated. The words: 'Made in the last Promotion of the *Blest*' can be taken perfectly seriously. Yet they invite us to think of death and the soul's reception into Heaven in terms of official advancement, in a military, ecclesiastical or civil hierarchy, which are faintly inappropriate. I think there is little doubt that Dryden's turn of phrase is touched with irony which is very slightly comical: the notion of the saved souls being 'promoted' in batches is put forward with a grave smile; and when the magnificent first stanza has run its course and Dryden has thoroughly established the feeling about her, not as one of the local girls, but as an immortal soul, he returns to this note as he comes to her poetry and pictures her before her death as being 'on probation':

K

When thy first Fruits of Poesie were given,
To make thyself a welcome Inmate there;
While yet a young Probationer,
And Candidate of Heaven.

He covers this smiling image with the general tone of the baroque manner so that he does not seem to be actually making fun of her.

The second stanza, tracing the progress of the soul of Anne Killigrew through its previous tenements, Homer, Virgil, Sappho and the Rev. Henry Killigrew, is at first sight in the vein of the most absurd convention of high-flown compliment though it is not quite as absurd, for the occasion, as it would be if written today. Moreover, Dryden has prepared us for the idea in the first stanza:

Hear then a Mortal Muse thy praise rehearse
In no ignoble Verse
But such as thy own voice did practise here.

This is surely playful. Dryden could not possibly be serious in suggesting that Anne Killigrew could have written anything approaching the superb bravura passage with which his ode begins. But, as the author of a dedicatory ode, he can pay her the compliment of pretending that it is possible. The main thing is that Dryden is not *only* playing, which would be out of place in the circumstances. He is seriously proposing the theory of the unity of the world of literature. The myth of the progress of the poet's soul does not simply mean that the soul which just now occupied the 'beauteous frame' of Miss Killigrew was the same which once filled the frames of Homer and Virgil—it has rolled through 'all the mighty poets' and it rolls still through all the true poets whether mighty or not, including Dryden himself. The soul which animated Virgil might by corollary be one which had animated previously some ancient Anne Killigrew. Minor poet or great poet, the spirit of poetry is one; and the last line stresses this:

Return, to fill or mend the Quire of thy Celestial kind.

It is as a member of the choir that she can be said to inherit the spirit of Homer and of Sappho without being a poet of their rank.

Stanza three combines the notion of the confraternity of Art with that of the confraternity of Christendom. The elevated feeling, the long complex rhythmic sentence with its exulting energy and the baroque exaggeration with a slightly comic undertone are maintained. The picture of the angels too busy celebrating Anne's birthday to work the usual miracles is obviously humorous, yet

> *And if no clustering swarm of* Bees
> *On thy sweet Mouth distilled their golden Dew*

is both serious and exquisite, so that it does make us feel that Dryden is perfectly serious about poetry and in saying that Anne has a place in it. All the same there is, I think, a deliberate lowering of tone from stanza one through stanza two and stanza three—a continuous and skilful modulation. Dryden is, in fact, bringing his poem down from heaven to earth and he has to get down to earth because he is now approaching the touchy part of the job: that of describing Anne's actual achievements. After this high-flown praise he is in danger of having either to contradict himself or to be insincere. He does neither. He chooses the one thing he can unreservedly praise, the innocence and purity of her verse, and he introduces this with a tirade on himself and the other poets writing for the contemporary stage. He would not have expected his readers to have taken him too literally, yet it may have been fitting. Dryden had been converted to the Roman Catholic Church the year before. He was engaged in writing *The Hind and the Panther*. He had given up writing for the stage for the time being. His cast of mind at the time was serious and preoccupied with questions of religion. There is no reason to doubt his sincerity. Yet it is difficult to feel that the repentance, however sincere, can be unmixed with irony.

What can we say t' excuse our Second Fall?
Let this thy Vestal, *Heav'n, atone for all;*
Her Arethusian *Stream remains unsoil'd,*
Unmixt with Forreign Filth and undefil'd,
Her Wit was more than Man, her Innocence a Child.

One can imagine neither that Dryden seriously thought the immorality of the Restoration stage equivalent to the Fall of Man itself, nor that he was unaware of the blasphemy involved in carrying on the comparison to the point where Anne Killigrew represents the central figure in a second Atonement for Sin. The comparison cannot be taken quite seriously, though the notion of the prostitution of the sacred arts of course can and indeed must be. In any case 'the steaming Ordures of the stage' presents so gross an image that it would be wholly out of place if Dryden was to be taken here as maintaining a really high and serious tone. And there must be irony, too, in 'Her Wit was more than Man, her Innocence a Child'. Not only do Anne's few immature poems do nothing that anyone could take seriously as redressing, let alone atoning for, the whole Restoration drama, but Dryden and his readers would be perfectly aware that literature is produced not by innocence but by experience. What he is doing here is broadening the ironic tone and in a sense coarsening the effects in preparation for his next stanza.

Art *she had none, yet wanted none,*
For Nature did that Want supply;
So rich in Treasures of her Own,
She might our boasted Stores defy:
Such Noble Vigour did her Verse adorn,
That it seem'd borrow'd, where 'twas only born.

Dryden, as his critical writings show, knew perfectly well that Nature does not and cannot 'supply' lack of art. At best it can do something to compensate for the lack. What he appears to be saying here is very like what he said of John Oldham's unskilful versification, that Anne's poetry was artless stuff but had a certain natural vigour and charm. The same is true of his treatment of her love poetry.

> Ev'n Love (for Love sometimes her Muse exprest),
> Was but a Lambent-flame which played about her Breast;
>   Light as the Vapours of a Morning Dream
> So cold herself, whilst she such Warmth exprest,
>   'Twas Cupid bathing in Diana's Stream.

Under the exquisite image, the sympathetic evocation of the Morning Dream cut off so soon, the comment is clear: her love poems show that she did not really know what she was talking about.

Next he turns to her paintings with a return to hyperbole, but without the tone of elevation. The exaggeration is good-humoured and jolly and has an overtone of the condescension with which one may praise amateur efforts without implying that they are good:

> Born to the Spacious Empire of the Nine,
> One wou'd have thought, she should have been content
> To manage well that Mighty Government;
> But what can young ambitious Souls confine?

There is a good-humoured chuckle in that 'One wou'd have thought', and Dryden hardly bothers to conceal it in his description of her paintings:

> Her pencil drew whate're her Soul design'd
> And oft the happy Draught surpass'd the Image
>   in her Mind.

That he hints her success to have been a somewhat hit-or-miss affair, the following lines describing her subjects leave little doubt. The tone and movement of the verse, with its jog-trot of octosyllabic couplets, is one of tolerant amusement. The subjects of her sketches are those with which talented young ladies have always filled romantic sketchbooks.

The Sylvan *Scenes of Herds and Flocks*
And fruitful Plains and barren Rocks,
Of shallow Brooks *that flow'd so clear,*
The bottom did the top appear

And so on. The concluding comment is open enough:

So strange a Concourse ne'er was seen before,
But when the peopl'd Ark the whole Creation bore.

   In fact this part of the poem descends to parody, though
parody of the gentlest kind. It must seem odd to find Dryden
breaking the accepted form of his ode, the irregular Pindaric
stanza, at this point and introducing a passage of descriptive
octosyllabic couplets. But readers of Anne Killigrew's volume
would recognize that he here breaks into an imitation of her
own style in her poems describing her pictures. For example
that entitled 'On a Picture Painted by her self, representing
two nimphs [sic] of DIANA's, one in a posture to Hunt, the
other Batheing'.

We are Diana's Virgin-Train
Descended of no Mortal strain;
Our Bows and Arrows are our Goods,
Our Pallaces, the lofty Woods,
The Hills and Dales, at early Morn
Resound and Eccho with our Horn;
We chase the Hinde and Fallow-Deer,
The Wolf and Boar both dread our Spear;
In Swiftness we out-strip the Wind
An Eye and Thought we leave behind

And so on and so on. This strain is continued in the next
stanza on Anne's royal portraits:

Our Phenix queen was portrai'd too so bright,
Beauty *alone cou'd* Beauty *take so right:*
Her Dress, her Shape, her matchless Grace
Were all observ'd as well as heav'nly Face.

The manner is one of the highest and most enthusiastic praise, but it hardly fits with what Dryden is actually saying. It is no compliment to a really competent artist to tell him that he has the shape right in a portrait, that the face is recognizable and that he has made no mistakes in the portrayal of the costume. To regard this as praise is to imply that the painter is an amateur or a tyro. The irony here is hardly disguised at all:

What next she had design'd, Heaven only knows:

With this stanza the modulation of the tone brings the poem to its lowest level, but the descent has been so skilful and discreet that there is no apparent incongruity with the elevation of the opening passage.

From this point Dryden begins to build up again. He cannot, without impropriety, take the great tone again at once so he modulates as it were into another key. In stanza eight the tone is, to begin with, one of tenderness and sympathy as the poet brings her before us as a person. Indeed he moves from the royal portrait to the self-portrait that provided the original of the engraving. He reflects on the cruelty of Fate and the double outrage on this charming young creature not only deprived of life but—ravaged with smallpox which destroyed her beauty first. He compares her fate with that of the Matchless Orinda. By the end of the stanza he has moved from amusement to tenderness, from tenderness to pity and from pity to enthusiasm. The poem is on its way up from earth to heaven again. It rises there by way of a stanza of what might be called personal anecdote moving into myth: a simple, moving and charming description of her brother at sea not knowing of his sister's death and seeing a new star appear amid the Pleiades. From there it crashes into the great terminal passage where Dr Johnson smelt an inappropriate jest. It is, I think, not merely a joke, but it is certainly touched with the irony that runs through the whole poem. The irony is not merely in the image of the rattling bones filling the sky as they rush together but in the whole tremendous energy and speed of the Last Day. It is just as much in the picture of the Sacred Poets bounding from their tombs like a host of jack-in-the-boxes. And although it is comic, it is impressive and beautiful, because it has the energy and vigour of one of the great baroque pictures with the Saints soaring like heavenly rockets into the sky and the spectators portrayed in dramatic movement and a sweep of limbs and draperies that may be theatrical but is successfully and impressively theatrical. It is successful and impressive here because Dryden has *not* simply turned the Last Day into a gallop—he has suggested the enormous energy of Nature released and triumphant in its last hour— and in the same way, the picture of the sacred poets rocketing from their graves, though comical is not ridiculous, because Dryden makes it natural to the 'inborn vigour on the wing' which is the nature of poetry itself, the energy which is eternal delight. Nor is it exaggerated that Anne Killigrew should lead them into heaven. Dryden is not being at all ironical here. He is returning to the theme of innocence: 'And a little child shall lead them.'

The most important thing about the ode is usually missed: its superb modulation of tone. Johnson missed this perhaps —perhaps not: 'All the stanzas indeed are not equal. An imperial crown cannot be one continued diamond; the gems must be held together by some less valuable matter.' But he was aware of the other supreme quality that makes him call it an imperial crown: its triumphant energy—he seems to have been so conquered by this 'inborn vigour on the wing' that he does not treat the ode with the ruthless logic and common sense which it will no more bear than will 'Lycidas':

> Passion runs not after remote allusions and obscure opinions. . . . Where there is leisure for fiction there is little grief. . . . In this poem there is no nature for there is no truth, there is no art for there is nothing new . . . with these trifling fictions are mingled the most awful and sacred truths. . . . He who thus grieves will excite no sympathy; he who thus praises will confer no honor. . . .

All these strictures might be applied to Dryden's ode, and sometimes with more justice than to 'Lycidas'. In both cases there would be *some* justice at least—'Lycidas' has some incongruities, some 'fictions' which are hard to reconcile with the ostensible subject and the chosen form. Dryden's ode challenges taste, affronts propriety and common sense, and trembles on the edge of travesty throughout—one slip in the superb management and it would be merely ridiculous; the slightest falling off of the vigour and power and it would be simply theatrical and rhetorical. And the question arises: why, if we grant all the strictures that Johnson did make in the one case and could have made in the other, why is each still a marvellous poem? In each case it is the pure and exquisite feeling for the language triumphing over and justifying the mannerisms. Milton has chosen an effete pastoral style and made it lucid and vital, Dryden has chosen a rhetorical and baroque style and by the plainness and energy of his diction has made it vigorous and lambent. By the seriousness of his theme, the celebration of poetry, he has redeemed and transfigured the triviality of its subject. So far Tillyard is right. He is wrong in supposing the trivial matter is mere padding and not an integral part of a theme that embraces the whole range of the art from the merest beginners to the supreme masters.

All for Love, or Comedy as Tragedy

THE division of the whole literature of man into two modes, comic and tragic, is at first sight an odd one. Aristotle, I suppose, is partly responsible, though he is not to blame, since he appears simply to have described the two existing sorts of drama in his day. As he found them, they were different in origin, in style, in subject and in the occasions they served. There was no other sort of drama worth classifying, so that comedy and tragedy between them took up the whole field. Having described the facts as he found them, Aristotle then went on to describe the distinctive characters of the two sorts of drama. It was largely the work of later ages to turn these descriptions into laws of nature.

For Aristotle the nature of an action was, in part, decided by the nature of the agents. In the tragedy of his day he found the characters represented as rather better than men are in real life, those in comedy rather worse. By better and worse he appeared to be making a moral distinction but it obviously was also a social one. Man is a rational animal. Every creature strives towards the perfection of its own nature. Man is born with his passions but his reason can only be brought to that perfection, and that control of his passions which alone makes him fully human, by education. Only the man perfected by education is fully human and only such men can undertake courses of action which we can take quite seriously. And, since man is a social animal, or, as Aristotle calls him, a political animal, the actions in which the superior man is faced with decisions affecting the state as a whole are more serious, of greater weight and beauty as actions than those which concern only private relations between individuals. This is the sphere of the tragic.

Below this level of action are those men who because they labour at mechanical trades, or because they suffer from defects of nature, or for other reasons, are never able to

144

reach the full fruition of their human natures and those who, limited in some way from participation in public affairs, are thereby excluded from the most serious kinds of action. So that behind the classification of drama into the tragic and the comic, there would appear to lie a similar possible classification of literature in general into the serious and the comic.

The gap in this system is, of course, a sort of literature (including drama) which would represent men as neither better nor worse than they actually are, but capable of being serious and comic at once. In spite of the fact that Christianity brought in a completely different view of human perfection and imperfection, drama on the whole continued to observe the Aristatelian division of serious and comic types of characters and their proper social standing until the novel appeared to treat its characters as they are in real life. Once it is admitted that the seriousness of human action is a matter to be decided by God and not by man, that all men are equal in the sight of God, and that the perfection of the human consists not in fulfilling its own nature but in escaping from and rising above it, then indeed the old distinction of comedy from tragedy seems to disappear and we are left with the division of actions into those with happy endings and those with unfortunate ones.

In this age, moreover, sometimes, without any intention of irony, referred to as the Age of the Common Man, there is apt to seem something snobbish in a distinction which asserts that only certain rare and superior men and women are in fact capable of tragic action and that the rest, however terrible their fates, can be no more than pathetic. The proper response to pathos is sympathy, an emotion that links us with those who are like ourselves at every level of nature, but the response proper to tragedy is pity, an emotion that links us with what is greater than ourselves because in one respect or another it represents what is the utmost the human can hope to attain to; and added to this response must be a concern for the human itself, which we may call fear, since it consists in awareness that the human at its height is so precarious, so vulnerable, so implicit with disaster.

I believe that the distinction described by Aristotle can be maintained and that all literature that represents men in action can be fruitfully divided into tragic and comic. But if the distinction is made between the tragic and the pathetic as I have suggested, if we take the comic to include all those cases of action where the agents are men of the inferior sort, together with those where the action itself is not *serious* in the full sense, the sense of testing the human to its limits, then it will be necessary to sort out many works of literature commonly regarded as tragedies and place them with the comedies, and to re-examine some reputed comedies and place them with the tragedies.

One such play is Dryden's *All for Love*. It was written with the avowed purpose of rivalling Shakespeare's *Antony and Cleopatra* and the comparison invited at the time has gone on ever since. Each in its way is a masterpiece but on the whole Shakespeare's play has usually been considered the better tragedy of the two. The comparison is perhaps unfair to Dryden's play because it is not, I think, an example of tragedy at all. It belongs properly to the class of what I would call pathetic comedy, as an examination of the play, with an occasional glance at Shakespeare's genuinely tragic drama, will demonstrate.

Dryden, of course, intended a tragedy, and a tragedy of a particular kind. In taking up 'this bow of Ulysses', he was not trying to write a period piece in imitation of a Shakespearian tragedy. There is no suggestion of pastiche. *All for Love* observes the unities in the Restoration manner. In spite of its generally plain and naturalistic dialogue, it has some touches of the *Heroick* plays of its period, and it is based on a different conception of tragedy from *Antony and Cleopatra*. Shakespeare's play presents us with a picture of things as they are. We can draw our own moral conclusions from the events. But for Dryden it is the business of the playwright to put the moral into the play, to show virtue rewarded and vice punished, and he praises the story as a subject for drama because of 'the excellency of the moral: for the chief persons represented were famous patterns of unlawful love; and their end accordingly, was unfortunate'. What Shakespeare thought about their end is not known but there is no hint in the play of moral condemnation. Antony has been stupid; Cleopatra has been irresponsible; both have been reckless but both have acted deliberately and with knowledge of the nature of their actions. They are fully answerable and the play ends on something very like a note of triumph, even of exaltation, which touches even the cold-blooded Augustus. This is just what worried Dryden. He feels that Shakespeare's play is imperfect as a tragedy, in Aristotle's sense:

> That which was wanting to work up the pity to a greater height, was not afforded me by the story; for the crimes of love, which they both committed, were not occasioned by any necessity or fatal ignorance, but were wholly voluntary; since our passions are, or ought to be, within our power.

It is in this attempt to provide the basis of a 'moral' tragedy that Dryden in fact loses the tragic altogether. Shakespeare's Antony is a desperate gambler but he knows what he is about. Dryden's is represented as so enslaved by love that he is barely responsible. In his blind infatuation he throws away not only his own chances and those of Cleopatra, but our respect, though he may keep our sympathy. He has been so successfully endowed with an alternative to necessity or fatal ignorance that he is like a hopeless drunkard unable to keep away from the bottle, yet always trying to reform. We must not blame Dryden for this. It is his interpretation of the story and it is as probable an interpretation as Shakespeare's. Love does take hold of some characters as drink or drugs do of others, and with similarly degrading results. The weakness of Dryden's argument, however, is that, if Antony is made to lose his wits and his will-power under the effect of love in order to seem less responsible and therefore more to be pitied, at the same time the alleged moral of the story is weakened and almost destroyed. The cause of his downfall is made to appear less 'a crime of love', adultery, than a sort of insanity. He needs a doctor, not a judge. As a matter of fact, what happens to Antony and Cleopatra has very little to do with 'crimes of love' at all. Had Octavia never existed, had Antony been as cosily and morally married to Cleopatra as anyone could wish, the quarrel with Caesar could as easily have happened over something else, and one feels sure that Antony and Cleopatra would have made the same blunders. Antony, faced with the choice of abandoning her to join Ventidius and the army, would have behaved just as foolishly. Cleopatra would have fled from the Battle of Actium through the same cowardice, and Antony would have followed her. The Egyptians would have deserted to Caesar just as readily when things looked desperate, and the so-called 'crimes of love' would never have existed. Dryden's moral is in fact no moral at all. He does not succeed in showing the effects of vice, and the play is weaker than Shakespeare's precisely where Dryden claims its superiority to lie.

Nor is Dryden much happier in his claim to have made the play more 'regular' than Shakespeare's, to have made 'every scene in the tragedy conducing to the main design'. It is true, of course, that he has. It is a masterly piece of construction. There is a beautiful symmetry in the balance of forces and the construction of the action so that the suspense is continually being built up, the balance of fortunes becomes each time a little more precarious, and the final ruin comes with a sense of inevitable development. But to do this the springs of action must be placed elsewhere than in the two principal characters. The situation with which the play opens, with Caesar besieging the capital of Egypt after the Battle of Actium, Antony estranged from Cleopatra because of her desertion, and ruin facing both, is doubtless the result of their previous actions. But at this point the power to initiate further action has passed from them. Antony can do nothing to retrieve his position; he has lost his army and is helpless. Cleopatra can do nothing to win back Antony; she has nothing to offer him that he does not

already possess. Initiative and choice, the power to determine the course of events, are no longer theirs, and, in fact,
they never recover it. All they can do is to interfere with
what others determine and initiate. The real active powers
in the play, the initiators and actors, are Alexas the eunuch
and Ventidius, and they use Antony and the queen as pawns
in their game.

Consider the course of the plot: Antony at the beginning,
as we have said, is incapable of action. He is presented as a
sad, defeated figure like Richard II at Pomfret Castle, luxuri-
ating in his grief, throwing himself rather dramatically on
the ground, threatening melodramatically to kill anyone who
disturbs his orgy of self-pity, and even attended by a concealed orchestra to set his woes to music. Alexas wants to
save Egypt and himself by betraying him to Caesar, but
cannot because Cleopatra dotes on Antony still and if he
betrays Cleopatra he will perish himself. He is therefore
compelled to try to reconcile them. Then Ventidius arrives
and brings Antony back to himself by the news of the twelve
legions in Syria ready to serve him if only Antony will abandon Cleopatra, under whom they refuse to serve. Antony,
with some trouble, is brought to agree. But all the force of
the decision comes from Ventidius. The only active part that
Antony takes is his decision to say goodbye to Cleopatra
after being persuaded not to. In the same way it is Alexas,
the palace eunuch, who finds Cleopatra inert and in despair
and spurs her on to win Antony back; and of Antony he says:

> —I, who bear my reason undisturbed,
> Can see this Antony, this dreaded man,
> A fearful slave, who fain would run away,
> And shuns his master's eye: If you pursue him,
> My life on't, he still drags a chain along
> That needs must clog his flight.

Alexas is unfortunately right, and it is Alexas who makes the
plan and persuades her to it. If Ventidius is the master of
Antony, Alexas is the master of Cleopatra. They are in fact
like two chess-players moving their pieces on the board. They

have to act according to the known value and power of the pieces and to act through them, but it is they who plan the strategy and decide the moves. The real weakness of the figure of Antony as a tragic figure is not, as Nichol Smith suggests, that we do not, as in Shakespeare's play, first see him great and then fallen; it is that his decisions never depend on himself. Ventidius pulls him one way, Cleopatra another, and Octavia another. Much the same is true of Cleopatra.

The title of the play is *All for Love or the World Well Lost, A Tragedy*. Dryden seems to have considered that his two principles had deliberately chosen to sacrifice position, honour and life for love, and that in the nobility of this choice the tragedy consisted. But they never really weigh one thing against another; they never have a chance to decide for themselves even so far as they do. It is the game of pull-devil, pull-baker between Alexas and Ventidius which really determines the course of events, and they are the two persons in the play to whom love as alternative to worldly power is a meaningless choice. Ventidius is a soldier who takes a contemptuous view of love and thinks of Cleopatra as a nuisance and Antony's infatuation as criminal folly and nothing more. Alexas actively resents the love he cannot share.

> She dies for love; but she has known its joys:
> Gods, is this just, that I, who know no joys,
> Must die because she loves?

The world is in fact not well lost for love, it is not lost for love at all but because a eunuch wants to save his skin. He wins Antony back from Ventidius. Ventidius gets him back by using Octavia and the children. Alexas counters by persuading Cleopatra to flirt with Dolabella and get Antony back. But Antony, though he discovers the plot, will not believe it. Octavia and Dolabella, the two chief dangers to Alexas, are banished, but so is Cleopatra, who tries to kill herself. At this point, just as Alexas is preparing a countermove, the whole thing is overtaken by an accident, the desertion of the Egyptian fleet. It is Alexas's lie about Cleopatra's suicide which causes both deaths, but once the fleet was gone their fates were sealed in any case. From beginning to end neither Antony nor Cleopatra has the initiative which would give importance to their choices. As far as the action is concerned they are pathetic; to be tragic is not within the power of either.

In Shakespeare's play, Antony does some silly things and Cleopatra some irresponsible things. But the initiative of action rests with them throughout. We have a real battle between the values of love and the values of empire. Antony may be, as Octavius calls him, an 'old ruffian', but he is a self-made and self-propelled ruffian, not a puppet of politicians. Like Cleopatra he makes his own decisions and the play has tragic force.

This does not mean that Dryden's play is a failure. Far from it. But it is a pathetic comedy as far as its action is concerned and we can only accept its title if we take it as ironical. Taken as the tragedy Dryden intended, it is a bad play and satisfies the demands neither of art nor of morality. Taken as a comedy it satisfies all the requirements of comedy.

On the score of character much the same is true, and Dryden is no less unfortunate in the comparison. *Antony and Cleopatra* is a play based on a genuinely tragic opposition of values to be decided by a choice having the seriousness of a public action of the utmost moment. This opposition of values arises from the claims of two different views of life, two worlds whose values are absolute, undeniable, and in the circumstances irreconcilable. To grasp the nature of the claims and the implications of the choice demands characters of superior intelligence and real greatness of spirit; to make the choice demands an heroic act of will only to be found in persons with the rare quality of magnanimity; for magnanimity requires not only personal capacity for it, but the position in which the public and the private virtues can be exercised to the full. It is this that makes *Antony and Cleopatra* tragic. The two principals have the nobleness of nature to match the choice demanded of them. What makes

L

All for Love essentially a comedy is not that the principals lack nobility but that their choice depends on no real opposition of values. The action proceeds from the opposition only of two sorts of *demand* based merely on personalities and practical ends. There are no fundamental issues raised at all, though Dryden would like us to think there are. In Shakespeare's play we are made to feel the passion of Antony and Cleopatra as a beautiful, powerful, intense but principally an *absolute* thing. With the values of that passion it is not possible to compromise even when the Empire and life itself are at stake. But we are also made to feel that these two people are princes, they have the habit and outlook of kingship, they have and exercise responsibility for the *res publica*, the whole order and maintenance of society. For them, and they know it, a personal choice is also a public choice and all issues are double issues. The values imposed by their position are also absolute and imperious and, if conflict arises, reject the idea of compromise with personal desires; and these values have their own beauty. Human love appears to them and to us as a supreme power but a dangerous and disruptive force. In the end it is a clash between the values of an inner personal world of the spirit and the demands of the external world of society.

Shakespeare's play constantly balances one scene, in which we feel the force and importance of the external world, against one in which we feel the compulsion of the inner personal world. Whichever way the decision had gone we would have had a great tragedy. But, as I suggested before, we have the greater of two possible tragedies because we have the greater of two possible choices. Even Octavius recognizes it, and this and his ability to do so gives him a measure of greatness at the end of the play which he did not possess before:

> *Take up her bed*
> *And bear her women from the Monument,*
> *She shall be buried by her Antony,*
> *No grave upon the earth shall clip in it*
> *A pair so famous: high events as these*

Strike those that make them . . .
. . . . Come Dolabella, see
High order, in this great solemnity.

But in *All for Love* this conflict between two sets of values is hardly present at all. It is replaced for the most part by a conflict for possessions. Cleopatra treats Antony like an object which she wins or loses, a possession to which she clings as a possession. Shakespeare's Cleopatra is jealous of Octavia but it is a passionate jealousy not a possessive one. Dryden's Cleopatra, like everyone else in the play, is intriguing for the possession of Antony, and her love is a means to possession. In Shakespeare love is a way of life which is opposed to another way of life. In Dryden love is the rival of Empire in another sense; it is itself a sort of Empire, a possession to be lost or won, to be counted, assessed, bargained for and enjoyed.

When one compares the two plays one is struck by something that can only be called a middle-class commercial tone in *All for Love* which constantly comes out in the language of the principal people. For example, Act II:

IRAS: *Let it be past with you:*
             Forget him, madam.
CLEOPATRA: *Never, never Iras.*
         He once was mine; and once, though now 'tis
           gone,
         Leaves a faint image of possession still.

With this we may compare Antony's fine speech to Cleopatra when he decides to take farewell and goes over his points of complaint against her. Yet fine as it is, it takes the form of a profit and loss account. It has the tone of the manager of the bankrupt firm going through the books with a defaulting cashier, and Cleopatra's reply is perfectly in tone. She clinches it by proving that she could have sold out Antony to Caesar, but has in fact turned down a big offer from the rival firm. Antony gives in; recasts the accounts:

ANTONY: *My eyes, my soul, my all!* (embraces her)
VENTIDIUS: *And what's this toy,*
            In balance with your future, honour, fame?
ANTONY: *What is't, Ventidius?—it outweighs them all*
            .   .   .
            Faith, honour, virtue, all good things forbid,
            That I should go from her, who sets my love
            Above the price of Kingdoms! give, you gods,
            Give to your boy, your Caesar,
            This rattle of a globe to play withal,
            This gew-gaw world, and put him cheaply off:
            I'll not be pleased with less than Cleopatra.

So when, later, Antony remarks of Octavius:

> *Nature meant him for a usurer*
> *He's fit indeed to buy and conquer Kingdoms.*

he makes a good point but not as good a point as Dryden perhaps intended. For if Octavius is a usurer, Antony is a spendthrift on whom the usurer is foreclosing. The tone of business competition is accentuated. It comes out even more clearly in the famous scene in Act III where Octavia springs her emotional booby-trap on Antony—for it is little more than that. The children are used to soften him up and then she makes her generous offer to buy him back. It is very much the same technique that Cleopatra used in the previous act with her charming presents and the 'don't-you-remember-how-happy-we-were-together-darling' tactics. Each of the girls has her own set of hooks, and each plunges them into the carcass and pulls. When Octavia wins by the Mum-and-Kiddies ploy, Antony breaks into commercial language again. He gives himself back and distributes himself like a bonus to the defrauded shareholders:

VENTIDIUS: *Was ever sight so moving? Emperor!*
DOLABELLA: *Friend!*
OCTAVIA: *Husband!*
BOTH CHILDREN: *Father!*
ANTONY: *I am vanquished: take me*

> *Octavia; take me children; share me all.*
> *I've been a thriftless debtor to your loves*
> *And run out much in riot, from your stock;*
> *But all shall be amended.*

It is almost like a scene where the bankrupt compounds with his creditors and promises to pay nineteen and six in the pound.

And though the end of the play rises well above this tone, it never really recovers from it and it never really loses it.

Even in his great scene with Ventidius at the end it comes into Antony's language, if not his feelings:

> *O Ventidius*
> *What should I fight for now?—My queen is dead.*
> *I was but great for her; my power, my empire*
> *Were but my merchandise to buy her love;*
> *And conquered Kings my factors.*

One need not press the metaphor—but one cannot imagine it even occurring to Shakespeare's Antony: when he thinks her false he says:

> *. . . here I am Antony*
> *Yet cannot hold this visible shape, my knave.*
> *I made these wars for Egypt, and the Queen,*
> *Whose heart I thought I had, for she had mine:*

And later, when he hears she is dead

> ANTONY: *Dead then?*
> MARDIAN: *Dead.*
> ANTONY: *Unarm, Eros, the long day's task is done*
> *And we must sleep:*

It is impossible not to feel the difference between such passages.

This commercial note that sounds throughout, the emphasis on possessions rather than on powers and positions perhaps reflects a real difference in the structure and values of society between Shakespeare's day and Dryden's. In any case, it indicates a shift from the world of public affairs to the world of private life. *All for Love* is a comparatively bourgeois and domestic play. Antony and Cleopatra behave much more like private persons and less like people who by position and habit are public figures, the embodiments of state and the vessels of power. Cleopatra suffers from it more than Antony, who has his moments of authority and never entirely loses the tone of command.

Shakespeare's Cleopatra is essentially a woman, at times indeed a devastating picture of the uninhibited female of the species—but she never ceases to be a queen, as even her enemy Enobarbus bears witness:

> *I saw her once*
> *Hop forty paces through the public street*
> *And having lost her breath, she spoke and panted,*
> *That she did make defect perfection,*
> *And breathless power breathe forth.*

It is this power to make defect perfection and itself breathe forth power which Dryden's Cleopatra lacks. She fascinates no one but Antony, though everyone else bears witness that she has the power to fascinate. Dryden does try to make her a queenly figure, but she remains on one side a middle-class charmer, or at least nothing but Antony's little bit of fun, shrewd, wheedling, self-justifying and possessive. Indeed, she puts the domestic note very well herself:

> *Nature meant me*
> *A wife, a silly harmless household dove,*
> *Fond without art and kind without deceit . . .*

Of course she is deceiving herself as to her real nature, or perhaps adopting a pose. But in a sense she is perfectly right. She was not meant to be a queen but a private person—not a wife perhaps but someone's fancy-girl, the clinging vine of some suburban Antony. On the other side, Dryden obviously means her to be a figure of fatal passion, a tigress in love,

> *Vénus toute entière à sa proie attachée.*

But, as we have seen, he succeeds less in giving us a picture of the magnificent beast of prey than one of a venereal tycoon hanging on to her amatory bank-balance. Her character, in spite of a certain charm and appeal, is the essential material of comedy. Antony's is less so but his position in the play is, as we have seen, to be pushed to and fro, to be won and lost by the real agents; his traits are noble but his role is essentially comic, and the play is ironic and pathetic rather than tragic in its effect.

A test of the difference between the two plays is the relationship between Antony and Cleopatra in each. Both plays give a convincing and beautiful picture of love: passionate love in the case of Shakespeare's play, obsessive love in Dryden's. Dryden's two characters, aware of their fatal obsession, are seen struggling in its toils but helpless to break it. Shakespeare's characters, in spite of quarrels and misunderstandings, really seem to enjoy themselves; they are elevated and rejoice in the natural vigour of their passion. Dryden's Antony is never a match for his Cleopatra. He can cope with her no more than he can with Caesar, and in trying to do both he seems pathetic and ineffectual. At the end his tone is still anxious as he makes sure she will follow him:

> ANTONY: *Thou say'st, thou wilt come after: I*
>   *believe thee;*
> *For I can now believe whate'er thou sayest,*
> *That we may part more kindly.*

And he is resigned to make the best of things:

> *Think we have had a clear and glorious day*
> *And Heaven did kindly to delay the storm,*
> *Just till our close of evening. Ten years' love,*
> *And not a moment lost. . . .*

Of Shakespeare's Antony we do not feel that he is weak, though we see he has weaknesses. He is much more of a match for Cleopatra and much more of a match for Octavius too. Octavius is a great man, but he is a great man com-

157

THE CAVE AND THE SPRING

mitted entirely to the values of the public world whose crown is power and rule. Cleopatra is a great woman, but committed entirely to the private world whose crown is personal love. Each of them is incomplete because each solves the problem by denying one side of it. Antony is in one sense caught between the two worlds and so ruined, but in another sense it is he who comes out of it best of all, for he alone has the power of knowing the fullness of life. His last words are an expression not of resignation, like the last words of Dryden's Antony, but of triumph in *both* worlds. Antony, when Eros has killed himself and he is about to do the same, does not look back with mournful satisfaction, like Dryden's Antony, to the treasure of love he must leave behind; there is no dying fall in the music:

ANTONY: *Thrice nobler than myself,*
Thou teachest me, Oh valiant Eros, what
I should, and thou couldst not. My Queen and Eros
Have by their brave instruction got upon me
A nobleness in record. But I will be
A bridegroom in my death, and run into 't
As to a lover's bed.

And when he dies his thoughts do not dwell like Dryden's Antony on his failures:

My fortune jades me to the last; and death
Like a great man, takes state, and makes me wait
For my admittance—

He recognizes defeat but not failure, and speaks proudly to Cleopatra:

The miserable change now at my end,
Lament nor sorrow at: but please your thoughts
In feeding them with those my former fortunes
Wherein I lived the greatest Prince o' th' world,
The noblest: and do now not basely die,
Not cowardly put off my helmet to
My countryman. A Roman, by a Roman
Valiantly vanquish'd. Now my spirit is going;
I can do no more.

This is the interesting thing about Shakespeare's Antony. In both the worlds, in both these realms of value, he dies with a sense of triumph and noble achievement. And this magnanimity in Antony brings out the real sense in which the play is tragic. Its sense, if I read it right, is to make us feel the human situation at its height. To catch the fullness of life demands that none of its demands be evaded, but it may also mean that they cannot be reconciled. To be human to the full, to be greatly noble involves inevitable defeat. But this defeat is in a sense a greater triumph than to save oneself by compromise. This is the heroic attitude: the attitude of mind one finds in heroic literature. Antony's life is an expression of the whole human situation. For we are all defeated in the end. We cannot beat circumstances. The choice before us is whether we assert absolute values in the face of circumstances or decide to come to terms with them. Antony at the beginning of the play sees the choice he may have to make and he makes it:

> Let Rome in Tiber melt, and the wide arch
> Of the rang'd Empire fall: here is my space,
> Kingdoms are clay: our dungy earth alike
> Feeds beasts as man; the nobleness of life
> Is to do thus.

The greatness of Shakespeare's Antony is that he chooses 'the nobleness of life' as he sees it, though he knows the consequences. The greatness of the play is that it makes us feel that he chooses rightly, that nobleness does take this risk and that if Antony fails it is in the sense that we all must fail if we refuse to compromise with life. Yet this sort of failure is the only way in which man remains undefeated: the nobleness of life is to do thus.

The attitude of Dryden's Antony at the end is very different. It almost amounts to saying: well, anyway, we had a good time while it lasted and that is the best we could hope for. This is not the heroic attitude and it is only the noble attitude in so far as it refuses to complain, looks facts in the face, and accepts them. But this is not meant to be quite

159

M

the tone of the play. Dryden, I think, really means to show the world well lost for love. He wants to show that love at its most intense is worth sacrificing all other goods for, even life itself. Antony's speech to Cleopatra at the beginning of Act III puts this view clearly:

> Receive me goddess,
> Let Caesar spread his subtle nets like Vulcan;
> In thy embraces I would be beheld
> By heaven and earth at once;
> And make their envy what they meant their sport.
> Let those, who took us, blush; I would love on,
> With awful state, regardless of their frowns,
> As their superior gods.
> There's no satiety of love in thee:
> Enjoyed, thou art still new; perpetual spring
> Is in thy arms; the ripened fruit but falls,
> And blossoms rise to fill its empty place;
> As I grow rich by giving.

This speech is interesting in several ways. It is one of the few places in the play where the typical high-flown language of the heroic plays is heard, and its occurrence marks the fact that Antony here has lost his sense of practical events. From the point of view of people like Ventidius he has temporarily lost his senses; he is in the delirium of passion and his language shows it. But Antony here is sane enough. He is asserting the other realm of values in which the world seems well lost for love. The theory implicit in this speech is that love is the supremely valuable thing in life because it alone enables men to transcend life on the ordinary practical level.

Antony is not entirely speaking in literary figures when he says that love makes them both gods. In other women there may, of course, be satiety, but the theory of transcendental love is that there *are* rare people in the world who, when they meet and fall in love, become invested with special powers and a special kind of experience; an experience in which time and change and decay are defeated. Ordinary love and ordinary lovers are not on this plane. But for those who have this gift, the gift must be used and nothing else must stand in its way; nothing else matters. It is like genius; its values override all others. If the ordinary demands of practical wisdom, or ordinary morality or even ordinary common sense conflict with the demands of this remarkable gift, so much the worse for them. This doctrine of the amatory *Übermensch* is a common feature of the heroic drama. *All for Love* is not an heroic drama, it is a realistic study of men in the real world and it shows the inevitable result of adopting the theories of the heroic drama in the actual world. Dryden's Antony is like Don Quixote charging the windmills. Shakespeare's is more like Roland holding the pass at Roncevalles. Shakespeare's undertakes a desperate gamble, but he does it with his eyes open. He too has a view of love of a special kind which it is the gift of special people to use to the full:

> *The nobleness of life*
> *Is to do thus: when such a mutual pair,*
> *And such a twain can do 't, in which I bind*
> *On pain of punishment, the world to weet*
> *We stand up peerless.*

But it is a humanist and not a transcendental view. Love does not raise him above human nature: it does not make him a god. But it does raise him to the very heights of which human nature is capable. This is what he feels and this is why when he is put to the test he chooses love and not empire, though he does not give up empire till he has done all short of sacrificing love to it.

For all this, Dryden's Antony cannot be said to have a false or deluded idea of love. Don Quixote was not deluded about the ideals of chivalry. He was only deluded about the world in which he wished to put them into practice. He was deluded about windmills, not chivalry. Dryden's Antony is not deluded about the transcendental nature of love, he is deluded about the nature of Cleopatra. Love is like, let us say, literary genius. Everybody can use words and many people can use them very effectively. But there occur in the world certain rare people who can use the same ordinary words in a way that causes them to fuse and flash out with what Coleridge called *esemplastic power*, and then we have the miracle of great poetry. Words so used have a new quality, unique, unanalysable and one for which there is no recipe, something that transcends the ordinary qualities of words however skilfully combined, as the qualities of a diamond differ from those of charcoal or black lead. Yet the diamond is only carbon. Nearly all human beings have the power of love and many of intense passion. But there are types of persons who when they meet and fall in love produce a new quality of experience, a new power of being which transcends ordinary experience as great poetry transcends ordinary powers of language. Had Dryden's Antony and his Cleopatra been people of this sort, had he been able to make us enter into their realm of experience as the poet can make us enter into the world of poetry, the play would have been a great tragedy. It might have been greater than Shakespeare's, for it would perhaps have raised greater issues. But, as we have seen, neither of the principal characters is of this sort. Dryden's Antony is at bottom a sentimentalist in love. He is not a man raised above himself by love, for love is something he simply gives way to. And when he gives way to it he seems to us a weakened and diminished character. He is a love-addict as some people are whisky-addicts. Cleopatra, for all her charms and graces, her unswerving and tenacious will and her indomitable courage, has something rather vulgarly feminine about her, too much of the 'little woman' conscious of her charming wiles—the sort of thing which is perfectly expressed by Ventidius's exclamation as he watches her practising her charms on Dolabella:

> *Woman, woman,*
> *Dear, damned, inconstant sex!*

These do not strike us as the sorts of people capable of the miraculous transformation of experience that love is sometimes capable of in those rare human beings who have the gift and the genius for it. There is too much of the temperament of the trader in their natures, too little of the temperament of the creative imagination. Now this is where Shakespeare succeeds. The one thing that marks off his Antony and his Cleopatra from all the other people in the play is this gift of imagination: whatever their faults and weaknesses, they have the temperament of genius. And like creative genius they have the power of transmitting their vision to others. Even the unimaginative and practical Octavius catches fire and shows a touch of it as he looks at Cleopatra dead:

> *She looks like sleep,*
> *As she would catch another Antony*
> *In her strong toil of grace.*

These are not the types whom Dryden has given us, but he has given us an extremely perceptive and true picture of other types; and what these types are can best be indicated by the analogy of poetic genius already employed. Poetic genius is rare. People who show no sign of it are the great majority. But in between there is a large number of people who show at least a touch of talent. The world is full of people who have the ability to *comprehend* the higher plane of experience that poetry presents, but who have not the gift for it, and a number of these people actually try to write poetry. Sometimes they touch it for a flash, here and there; but for the most part what they write falls dead from the pen. It has the form, the technical externals, the outward and visible form but not the inward and spiritual grace. This is the relation of Dryden's lovers to love. They do touch it momentarily as Antony's great speech shows. But on the whole they fail to convince us and, like the poetaster, they seem to mistake the imitation for the real thing. They mistake infatuation for passion and delirium for imaginative vision. It is this which makes the play essentially a comedy.

Literature versus the Universities

In 1958 I spent fifteen months of travel visiting universities in Canada, Great Britain, and the United States. Looking at the study of English in these universities I felt, as a Professor of English, that the subject was flourishing, the standards of scholarship and of criticism were higher than they have ever been before. Looking at them as a poet I found myself getting more and more uneasy, until uneasiness in the end grew into a kind of nightmare. Something very odd and probably very unpleasant is happening to literature, and if my examples are mostly drawn from the United States, that is only because the process has gone further there than elsewhere. The same sort of thing is happening all over the world. What is happening is what happened to the Sorcerer's Apprentice when, in his master's absence, he started the spell going, but did not know enough magic to stop the spell again.

The trouble all began, I suppose, when the universities introduced English literature as a subject and made it a staple of education—a function in which it very quickly ousted the classics from their traditional position. The Scottish universities began it in the eighteenth century. London University introduced it in England in 1859, though the chair of English had been established some years earlier. The older universities did not introduce the subject till near the end of the century. But outside the British Isles it seemed a perfectly natural subject to introduce into the Arts curriculum as new universities and colleges were founded. The fight against its introduction in England seems to us now rather foolish. A great and ancient literature surely deserves to be a subject of the highest and most serious study, and it is natural that it should be studied in the universities of the people who produced that literature. Those who thought

164

English inferior as a training in taste and critical acumen to the literatures of Greece and Rome argued so patently from prejudice, and overstated their cases so consistently, that they deserved to lose the fight. And yet when one sees what has happened to the university study of English literature, when one sees what it seems to be doing to the production of literature, one cannot help wondering whether it might not have been better if the prejudiced and the pigheaded had won the day.

The trouble started in the middle of the nineteenth century. Before that time some writers in every generation had received university educations, but on the whole there was not much association between literary men and scholars, and certainly no organized relations at all. And this state of affairs persisted even after English had become a subject of university study. Young men and women taking a course in the liberal arts or the humanities enjoyed for a few years the privilege of studying the literature of their own race under men who spent their whole lives at the same delightful and fairly leisurely occupation. As a fellow student of mine once said as we watched the Professor of English amble past: 'Fancy being paid to read what you like!' Unless the student intended to teach, English studies had no particular use, and there were so few teaching positions at universities and they were so poorly paid that on the whole only dedicated or devoted souls took up the subject as a career. Universities were few, and were on the whole only for the well-to-do. These were the conditions of the study of English literature at a university about the beginning of this century. Research and criticism in these conditions were carried on for their own sake and, for anyone who wanted to do original work, there were large areas of English literature still almost untouched. It was a common thing to carry the university study of the subject no further than the end of the eighteenth century, or at most to the death of Wordsworth in 1850. Living authors were left alone, though if they were very famous they might be invited to dine and visit the university, and have honorary degrees conferred on them, like Tennyson, or they might be elected to give some supernumerary lectures, like Matthew Arnold as Professor of Poetry at Oxford.

In the last fifty years all this has completely changed. The numbers of those who want a university education and can qualify for it have increased enormously, and will be increasing still more in the next fifty years, so that universities multiply and have tens of thousands of students where they once had hundreds. More and more it becomes necessary to have a university degree for any better sort of job. In the United States it is now almost the normal thing for most people with a secondary education to go on to a university, and this is becoming more and more the pattern all over the English-speaking world. This pressure in turn has meant that post-graduate work and higher degrees are the things that distinguish a man from the mass of graduates. In most of the colleges and universities of the United States today the trend is towards two or three years of general education to the level of the bachelor's degree, followed by training in the graduate schools. In this general education, English has become staple. There are about two and a half million students distributed over some two thousand institutions of higher learning in the United States. Nearly all of these students take a course in English somewhere in their study for a degree. This is big business. English ranks fifth among university subjects in the number of doctoral theses presented and accepted, and this reflects its importance and size in university education. Moreover its companions in the 'big five' subjects are Chemistry, Education, Economics and Physics. You have to go a long way down the list to find other subjects in the humanities. Universities now have a high prestige, and offer high rates of pay and good chances of advancement. English, from a new and not very utilitarian subject, has become a high-pressure industry.

In the first place it is obvious that an enormous number of university teachers is required. The time-honoured method is to pick those who qualify best in the university examinations. But the pressure of competition is so high that nobody

166

has much chance of appointment unless he can produce a doctoral degree, and this means a research thesis or dissertation on some aspect of English literature. Australia is a backward country; I found it very difficult to persuade people in Canada and the United States that I could be a Professor and head of a department in a university and not be Dr Hope. A little arithmetic will show that in order to staff American universities and colleges a very large number of pieces of research must be undertaken and written up. Those successful in writing doctoral theses will proceed to teach astronomical numbers of graduates who will all be doing research theses, and the teachers themselves, in order to improve their market value, will be expected to contribute articles to scores of learned or specialist journals and to publish books of research and criticism.

What has happened in consequence is a very curious reversal of the values of the last generation. A generation ago, research in the field of literature was undertaken in the interests of literature, to provide more knowledge, to provide good texts, to establish the canon of a writer's works, and to clear up misunderstanding by historical criticism. *Now* the purpose of nine-tenths of the research and criticism that goes on is to help the researcher to qualify in the great rat-race. The problem can be put in its crudest form by a few figures. A count of the English writers of even very moderate literary importance from the Venerable Bede to Robert Browning will give a muster of well under a thousand names. In one well-known history of English literature I made it 617. This is the field of material from which this great modern industry has to continue to produce 'original research' and original criticism. From 1940 to 1950, American universities and colleges accepted nearly two thousand doctoral theses, in the field of English—1,710 in fact. Heaven knows how many theses were written but not accepted. At the same rate in the next fifty years some ten thousand topics of research will be found and accepted in this small field of less than 1,000 authors worth investigating.

But in fact the rate of increase is from fifteen to twenty per cent every decade. At this moment in the United States about twelve to fifteen thousand topics of criticism and research are being pursued by graduate students, directed by highly trained teachers looking out for the slightest evidence of originality in a field already very well worked over. By the end of the century another three hundred thousand topics must somehow or other be found unless the whole system is to become a farce.

It is obvious that the whole thing is absurd. My concern, however, is not so much with what will happen as with what is happening now, and this is where I come to matters of concern to writers. After all, you may say, what do I care if the universities get themselves to the absurd point where there are ten million learned works about each original poet or novelist no matter how minor. Let the universities solve their own problems. It doesn't affect me as a writer if they produce separate studies on each syllable that Shakespeare wrote. Shakespeare is dead and it doesn't matter to him, and by the time they get round to you and me we shall be in the same state.

This I think is where you would be wrong. Because the situation quite clearly is affecting contemporary writers in Canada and the United States in two ways, both of which may be unfortunate for writing.

In the first place the immense pressure to find fresh material for research and criticism has meant that the field has been ransacked to its very dregs, and many writers better left forgotten have been dug up and become the subject of serious critical biographical and bibliographical studies. The effect is perhaps something like breeding back the unfit and the genetic misfits into a healthy stock. There is something very healthy for literature in the fact that the minor writers and the worthless writers tend to disappear without trace and only the great writers remain in the tradition and *as* the tradition. There is something dangerous for taste in keeping the trivial and the second-rate. For the body politic of literature, as for the body man, constipation is not a healthy state.

168

In the second place, the range of the English courses of the last century has been increased, and now tends to take in the whole field of living writers, and the whole field of writing in English: American, Canadian, Australian and so on. No sooner does a modern writer achieve some fame in the United States than his books are prescribed in university courses, his work becomes the subject of dozens of research theses and critical theses, and he himself is invited to write and lecture on his own creative processes. T. S. Eliot is an example of a writer who well before his death had an enormous number of books and articles devoted to his work and the tide is still rising. The actual quantity of Eliot's work, to say nothing of its quality, is extremely slight. The result of all this is that the modern writer writes in an atmosphere of critical inspection equivalent to that of a man trying to make love under a hundred arc-lights before a large and critical audience. He may manage to do it, but he will do it as a dramatic performance and he is much less likely to reach what Donne calls the 'right true end of love'. I believe that the same is true of that very private performance which produces poems, plays and novels.

Even so there is not enough material for the thesis industry. The research worker pursues the writer into his workshop. There is a minor industry in the United States in the gathering of the scraps of paper and drafts that writers produce on the way to the finished article. When I was approached a few years ago to act as Australian agent in collecting the 'work sheets' of Australian poets, I felt that the great academic machine was now hungrily breathing down the poet's neck as he wrote, and it would not be long before research began on the still unwritten works of living authors.

This is perhaps a little fanciful, but the general effects already observable are not fanciful. A serious study of the State of American Writers by Malcolm Cowley, president of the principal association of writers in America, came out in 1947. When I was in the country I met Mr Cowley, who confirmed his views of ten years before. The most important of these was the observation that, with the great prestige of English studies in American universities, literary criticism which had once been the handmaid of literature was fast becoming the mistress. In the last fifty years there has been a growing gap between literary writing and popular and amusement writing. Universities, by making the works of the 'literary' or 'high-brow' writers the subject of serious study and discussion, have made publishers and writers much more attentive to what academic critics have to say. As Cowley says:

> Even the new creative writing shows a high degree of critical consciousness—so much so that the novels and poems of the new age sometimes read like themes written to illustrate the best critical principles. Criticism has come to occupy such a central position in the literary world that it is hard to find historical parallels for the situation.

And he gives a number of examples of the ways in which writers tend nowadays to follow, not the fashions set by other writers who would have set the vogue in the past, but the fashions suggested by the latest literary theories. And it may be pointed out that the modern tendency for a critical theory to arise every year or so is itself not unconnected with the great thesis industry. Demand creates supply, and one obvious solution to the absurd problem of getting an infinite number of original theses out of a very small and finite number of poems, plays and novels, is to approach them with a new critical theory. Then the whole boiling can be reassessed in the light of the new theory, and so on *ad infinitum*.

The only objection to this is that, unless we agree that critical theories are trivial anyway, we shall have to agree that the number of possibly sound or even plausible theories is even more limited than the number of authors to whom they can be applied. Under the present system there is a premium placed on the odd, the extravagant, the intellectually perverse.

In any case, all I know of writing at first hand and at second hand suggests to me that real creative originality and the sources of literary imagination are imperilled by too much critical theorizing, and that writing to rules or to theories, however attractive, is apt to produce the kind of writing that has no real roots.

Another interesting point that Cowley has raised is that while in the past most writers learned their trade by the age-old process of solitary apprenticeship, more and more of them now take courses in creative writing at universities or colleges. A whole new industry and profession has grown up, that of the teacher of creative writing. I saw some of these courses in Canada and the United States, and I was impressed by what I saw. People really do learn to write poetry very capably, novels that sell, and short stories that pay handsome dividends, and not merely in the popular and glossy magazines. One director of the School of Creative Writing at Leland Stanford University told me that he gives a publishers' luncheon about once a fortnight, and that the work of his graduates—though he did not use the expression —sells like hot cakes.

At the same time I could not help feeling that there was something disturbing about the whole thing—a feeling that the universities are beginning to move in, take over, train and control writers—and that it will not be long perhaps before there are no wild writers left any more. In Canada, for example, I found that, more and more, it is not only in the universities that poets get their training, but in the universities that they can then get their living. No poet ever makes a living by poetry, of course. It is interesting to compare the way the living poets in two recent Penguin poetry anthologies, the Canadian and the Australian, earn a livelihood. Of fifty living poets represented in the *Penguin Book of Australian Verse* about thirty per cent work at some form of journalism, and only twelve per cent at teaching or research in English at a university. But in Canada, of forty living poets, thirty-five per cent are academic teachers of English.

This might at first sight seem not to be a bad thing, but in many cases I am sure that it is. Criticism, as many of the people

I talked to agreed, is a comparatively easy and a most interesting substitute for creation—it is, of course, at its best a genuinely imaginative and creative activity. But it means that the poet is tempted more and more to be a critic and tends to write less and less poetry. In addition the poet trained in a school of creative writing by academic critics and taking a job in the same atmosphere is more and more tempted to fall under the same influence that Cowley noted among the novelists—to produce work which, more or less unconsciously, is written in illustration of current critical theories; and thus reversing the proper order of nature in which the critical theories arise to deal with the independent raw material of the creative imagination. Yeats once made a sardonic comment on professors of literature:

> *Bald heads forgetful of their sins*
> *Old, learned, respectable bald heads*
> *Edit and annotate the lines*
> *That young men tossing on their beds*
> *Rhymed out in love's dispair*
> *To flatter beauty's ignorant ear.*

He is right: but there is nothing wrong with either process. This is the proper order of nature and the proper relation of writer and critic. What is really disturbing is when the young lover has the professor in bed with him and knows his performance is being graded as a first or second class honours, pass or fail. Writing is, or should be, a single-minded process. It may in the end prove as fatal for creative writers in America to get mixed up with the processes and ends of education and research as for the Russian writers to get mixed up with the processes and ends of the Marxist state. In the latter case the result has been a dreary mediocrity, the servile literary bourgeoisie who hounded Pasternak to his grave.

But the results, if the critical and educational machine captures the writers, are just as likely to end in formalism, triviality and mediocrity, and in servility of another kind.